WHEN *Good Enough* JUST ISN'T GOOD ENOUGH

Robert Leslie Holmes

AMBASSADOR INTERNATIONAL
Greenville, South Carolina • Belfast, Northern Ireland

When Good Enough Just Isn't Good Enough

Cover design & page layout by A&E Media — Rita Blajeski

ISBN 1 932307 40 0
Published by the Ambassador Group

Ambassador Emerald International
427 Wade Hampton Blvd.
Greenville, SC 29609
USA
www.emeraldhouse.com

and

Ambassador Publications Ltd.
Providence House
Ardenlee Street
Belfast BT6 8QJ
Northern Ireland
www.ambassador-productions.com

The colophon is a trademark of Ambassador

To Barbara and to the congregations we've
served together

CONTENTS

FOREWORD

When Good Enough Just Isn't Good Enough is an intriguing title—one that catches and holds the attention and opens the mind to the author's intended concept. The book is rich with explanations, enlightenment, and inspiration that encourage mankind and glorify God. Dr. Holmes gives enough historical background to draw our immediate interest. His easy-to-read style and obvious commitment to the message give it a sense of believability that is important to any reader, regardless of his or her background or experience. Best of all, whether a person knows Christ as Lord or is still searching, this book provides many answers that help the reader arrive at clear, informed decisions.

In this day of incredible changes at break-neck speed, Dr. Holmes assures us there is tremendous comfort in knowing that Christ is the same yesterday, today and forever. This realization brings peace and comfort to the believer and in our hurry-hurry, stress-filled world today this is a large benefit. His description of the validity of God's Word is simple and convicting. His easy, natural writing style enables the reader to understand and follow through on an organized progression of thought with clarity and simplicity.

Dr. Holmes has genuine regard for his fellow man, exceeded only by his love for his Savior, both of which are evidenced as he pours his heart out in this significant book. He openly shares his love for all sinners and his understanding that it is by the grace of God that all of us come to know Christ as Lord. His application of Biblical principles in his own life has enabled him to be a factor in bringing resolution to conflict in many situations. This book can help bring closure to some of the warring factions in your own life.

As you read and think your way through this book, you will become increasingly convinced that there are those occasions in all of our lives when we've settled for good enough, when in reality good enough just wasn't good enough. Holmes's dramatic demonstration of this fact is brought into clear focus as he concludes the book.

Knowing Dr. Holmes and having read some of his previous works, I can tell you that you are in for a treat—a life-changing one.

—ZIG ZIGLAR

PREFACE

Good! Better! Best! Three words it seemed I had known all my life but not in the way I was about to be introduced to them. Through a series of positively extraordinary events, I first became aware of the meaning of those three phrases in a new, exciting, and deeper way than ever before as a new immigrant to the United States in 1967. Freshly arrived in America, Sears, Roebuck, and Company was not my first choice in employment, but it was a lot better than I had expected. You see, I had qualified as a welder at the technical college in Belfast so that I could enter the United States under the then-current new immigrant quota system. I had been recruited to weld ship hulls, but through an oversight that I long ago decided was one of God's great preplanned blunders, my prospective employer informed me that I could not be employed for at least four months. What should I do? It had taken everything Barbara and I could gather to pay our airfares for ourselves and our ten-month-old son, Gary. Four months of vacation was out of the question. What would we live on? We were almost penniless. And, with no unemployment benefits available, the best plan was to find a job fast. So, in a new country with no job, I had gone knocking on the doors of prospective employers, none of whose names were familiar to me. In that context, I found myself with a job offer the same day from the biggest retail organization in the world.

Now, here I was and those three terms were being clearly enunciated to a rookie Sears employee on his first day at work. The "Good," I was informed, was really the mid-quality merchandise. "Anything below midline does not get a rating," the veteran leader of my initial training session told me. She went on to explain that "Better" was a designation for merchandise ranked about mid-way between "Good" merchandise and "Best." Products designated "Sears' Best" were the latest, most sophisticated on the market at that time. Sears often included the extra designation of "Sears' Exclusive," meaning the product was only available in a Sears, Roebuck and Company store. "Sears Best Exclusive is without doubt the hallmark of excellence," my instructor told me enthusiastically. I learned too that an ingenious double-barreled marketing strategy lay behind those labels. On the one hand, they helped customers to narrow their focus when buying something new. On the other, sales personnel knew that merchandise with a Better or Best designation often carried a bonus commission. It motivated us to go for the best, to strive for excellence every day we came to work.

Striving for excellence, is, in one sense, what this book is all about. But it is also about a lot more. In the pages that lie ahead, you are going to see repeated examples of why excellence is the only goal worth going after. There simply are no good substitutes for excellence, whether it's in your personal life or how you lead your organization. The opposite of excellence is something that none of us should ever want.

What is excellence? Well, let's settle one thing right away; excellence is not necessarily the same thing as perfection. Perfection and excellence are not synonyms. Excellence, said Booker T.

Washington, is to do ordinary things in an extraordinary way. He was right, of course. He might have added that excellence happens when ordinary people place themselves heart, soul, mind, and strength at God's disposal, whether it's in their personal life or in the things they produce. And excellence is never more important nor more desirable than when we seek to lead others. That is the foundational message of this book.

In late 1996 the elders of the historic First Presbyterian Church of Pittsburgh, where I was serving as senior pastor, met at the church's Ligonier Camp and Conference Center, in Pennsylvania's Laurel Mountains. We gathered to pray together and to design a new Mission Statement that would be a standard for doing Christ's work in the 21st Century. It was one of the most amazing retreats I have attended in more than 30 years of pastoral ministry. God's Spirit met us with power and the result was the Mission Statement that forms much of the framework for this book. When we met, we were convinced that God would not be honored by anything less than our best. Jesus said, *"Love the Lord your God with all your heart and with all your soul and with all your mind and with all your strength."* We knew that to give Him less than He asked for would be to short-change Him, and we were not there to do that. To give Him less or to try to buy God off with a substandard level of ministry would be not only to insult Him it would be clear evidence on our part that we, collectively, had lost sight of who He is. Therefore, we were resolved even before we began, that anything other than excellence for Christ would not be an option. The pursuit of excellence for Christ, so far as we were concerned, was our only option.

That retreat became a pivotal moment in the life of the congregation. As the principles set forth in these pages were put into play in the life of the church family, and especially among the leaders, new life came to a body of God's people who were looking for a new shot of the Holy Spirit. A fire was kindled within their hearts. The principles laid out in these pages have been tried and proven. Furthermore, I am convinced that they will work for you in your organization. That is not to say that they are the last word in church leadership, organizational renewal, nor in ordering your life, but they do provide a solid framework that is guaranteed to never fail when it is put into practice.

There is a difference between excellence and success. It is that success seeks to please people, while excellence seeks to please God. In fact, honoring God and serving Him better is the express goal of excellence as that word is used in these pages. Excellence calls for honoring God through self-improvement. It is about serving Him better tomorrow than you served Him today. By its very nature, then, excellence is always focused on the future. The goals we set for excellence become the road maps that guide us and show us the way into tomorrow.

While the Mission Statement referred to throughout the chapters that follow was developed expressly with one church in mind, much, if not all, of it can be adapted for use in your congregation. In fact, without too much work it can even be adapted for your personal life or business. After all, a church is not so much an organization as it is the extension of the sum total of the lives of its people. Much of what follows in these pages can be used to direct each of our lives in ways that please God. It is my hope and prayer that you will be inspired to examine the foundational tenets of this Mission Statement and own them for yourself and your church, or that you will find them a good starting place for developing a Mission Statement that helps you to serve Christ better where He has placed you.

In preparing these chapters for publication I have had three goals in mind. First, I wish them to honor God by inspiring you, my readers, to pursue excellence in all things. Even though these words are framed around the story of a church, they provide helpful suggestions and guidelines that can be applied to any organization. Second, I trust that they will become a source of encouragement for ordinary people who in their own lives desire to pursue excellence for Him who loved us all the way to Calvary. Third, I trust they will serve as a resource for other congregations or individuals seeking to find spiritual renewal and move forward into a new day of excellence for Christ's sake. If they achieve these goals then I am more than amply rewarded.

I dare not leave the reader with the idea that this is a one-man effort. Without the help of my friends, especially Betty Chapman, it would have been impossible for me to bring this project to completion. Debra Meyer brought her wonderful editorial skills to the task. Because of Debra, the standard of this work has been raised considerably. Thank you, Debra. My good friend, Dr. Richard Allen Bodey, read the manuscript and made helpful suggestions about both its theology and the expression of its content, as did my daughter-in-love, Catherine Holmes, who also helped with the index. I am grateful to them all. I'm especially thankful for the friendship of Zig Ziglar, whose printed and recorded words have served as a source of encouragement to me for many years. More recently, his personal friendship and encouragement is one of my life's great delights and blessings. Zig's Foreword is a treasure that I shall cherish for a long, long time.

Amy Browning, allowed me to use her home on the other side of the country in San Francisco as a retreat where in quietness and peace most of the final work for this little volume could be completed. We owe Amy, who was called home to heaven before this volume was published, a debt of gratitude for this and much, much more. My wife, Barbara, not only sacrificed a significant part of her vacation (in San Francisco, her favorite city, of all places) in order that I could give attention to refining this project, she read each chapter and made great suggestions that were adopted in each one. For her and to her there will always be due a special measure of love and gratitude.

The greatest teacher who ever lived, or ever will, Jesus, used parables constantly in His earthly ministry and no preacher can adequately tell Christ's story without illustrations. So far as is possible, I have tried to give credit where I have known the source for my stories. If I have unwittingly quoted someone without giving proper credit, please accept my apology and be assured that when I am notified of the omission I will give proper credit in any future editions of this work.

My prayer as I send this volume forth is that God will be pleased to use it to inspire His people to great new heights of excellence for His glory and to turn lives to the relentless pursuit of excellence for Christ wherever it goes.

—ROBERT LESLIE HOLMES
Summer 2004

MISSION STATEMENT

We stand steadfastly for:
Our Foundation . . . the Bible, God's Word;
Our Lord . . . Jesus Christ, God's only Son;
Our highest priority . . . to proclaim
Christ's cross and resurrection;
Our Highest Goal . . . that all may know
the saving power of the Gospel
and live a life worthy of Christ's calling;
Our Strength . . . The Holy Spirit.

Principles We Stand On

The Unchangeable and Non-negotiable Verities

Our Cornerstone: Jesus Christ!

Hebrews 13:8
*"Jesus Christ is the same yesterday
and today and forever."*

～〜

What is your life's cornerstone? What unchanging and unchangeable bedrock beliefs drive you? This question needs to be settled when we begin to pursue excellence in any organization. Hence it is the first primary focus of this book. *The Christian Century* magazine for November 6, 1996, carried this advertisement: "SENIOR MINISTER—Berkeley CA church seeks minister for local non-denominational congregation. Position open to Christians and non-Christians."

The closing sentence of that classified ad serves as an indicator of how far astray we in America have drifted in our mad quest for theological relativism. Many people are looking for a god (small "g") to meet their mood of the moment and who has no pre-set opinions or rules that stand in the way of their own designs on life. A plethora of new religious ideologies is presented to meet this shallow spiritual yen.

Add to this the fact that we live in days of overwhelming change. Who, especially in post 9/11 America, needs to be reminded of that? No matter where you live or work, you see the evidence of it all around you. When I spoke not long ago at the commencement exercises for one of the leading Christian colleges in western Pennsylvania, the president of the institution told me of a program that puts a new notebook computer in the hands of every entering freshman student. He reported that in one order for about 2,000 computers there were three upgrades, even though the same model number was listed on the invoice for all 2,000. Imagine, in that one shipment the computer model was upgraded three times. That is an indicator of how rapidly change is taking place in some parts of our world. Many of you know about change first hand. Not only computerization but foreign competition, global acquisitions, and corporate mergers have been calling, and will increasingly call us to adjust the way we live.

Against this backdrop I wrote the bedrock belief for a new Mission Statement for the church I was then serving. What is a Mission Statement? A Mission Statement is a succinct declaration of our reason for existing. It tells what we are about and, when properly done, ultimately becomes a good measuring rod against which we might measure how well we are doing. I presented my initial expression of a new Mission Statement for the church to its leaders during a fall retreat. There the elders received it for changes and adoption. A copy of the final product was published in church bulletins and newsletters over the next several months.

As I prayerfully contemplated my assignment, these words from Hebrews chapter 13 returned again and again to the forefront of my thinking: *"Jesus Christ is the same yesterday and today and forever."* If like me you find some change uncomfortable, I hope you will be encouraged again by this affirmation. It is the cornerstone of everything else in the Mission Statement.

"Jesus Christ is the same yesterday and today and forever." What does this Bible declaration mean? How does it instruct us? In this age of perpetual change it says that there is Someone with whom we can have a very personal relationship, both as a church and individually, who does not change. There is someone who is eternally reliable. That Someone is Jesus Christ our Lord.

WE CHANGE BUT CHRIST IS THE SAME

Our personalities and many important aspects of our character constantly evolve. Time changes us. Your portrait from years ago hangs on a wall in your home. It vividly tells the story of change. Every time we apply to renew our passports, the United States government requires new photographs. Why? The Passport Agency of our government knows that the 10 years between the issuance of one passport and the next often bring significant changes in our appearance. At times the changes are more evident than at others. For example, the picture on a baby's passport differs dramatically from the one sealed in that same child's passport when he or she is ten years old. On the other hand, the changes during mid-life may not be quite so pronounced, but they are real nevertheless.

As we reach life's later years, changes often are revealed in other ways. The eye which once flashed with fire may now be dimmed by many tears or framed with bifocals. Hair once plentiful and radiant red may now be scarce and gray. Face, form, and gait all testify to change. The mental portrait, could it be seen, would be even more telling. It would display opinions altered through new learning and new experiences. Priorities are often changed and temperaments softened by the hard experiences that shape our lives for our good, even though we may not realize it at the time. These experiences change the way we look at life, or even simply how we look. Affections cool too. Early life passions for people, places, and experiences often modify with time. Time does this to us; but time has no impact on the eternal Jesus.

It does not take years for changes to occur in us. Moods can transform our personality in an instant. We all know people who are like sweet peas one day and lemons the next. If you want to get along with them, you must first come just close enough to see what the temperament of the day is. This is never so with Jesus. He is never tired, never inconvenienced, never irritable, never moody, never unpredictable. He is always the same.

Attitudes change too. Not only that, but attitudes differ between people. Two brothers were eating grapes. One said, "Aren't these grapes the sweetest you ever tasted?" "Oh, I guess," said his brother, "but they're full of seeds." A bit later the first brother saw a flower seller. "Let's buy Mom a dozen of those beautiful red roses," he suggested. "No way! Their thorns might prick us and make us bleed," his negative brother replied. That evening they each were drinking some soda. "Mine is already half empty," griped the negative brother. "Mine is still half full," his positive peer replied with enthusiasm. Our attitude really can make a difference in how we perceive things.

Circumstances and experiences change us. Joseph, the son of Jacob, learned the hard way that a butler in prison will promise any favor, but will promptly forget it when he returns to the palace portico. Similarly, new power or wealth can alter us amazingly. Someone who in need and obscurity was approachable and genial becomes tyrannical and arrogant in affluence and ascendancy. Not Jesus, however! *"He did not consider equality with God something to be grasped, but . . . humbled himself and became obedient to death—even death on a cross!"*[2] He is the same Lord on heaven's throne as He was on Jerusalem's streets and Calvary's cross. Nothing will ever change Him.

Sin changes us. Our recognition of its presence in our own lives makes us either better or bitter. It softens our hearts through the acknowledgment of wrong or hardens them through an unwillingness to repent. We determine either to mend our ways or to keep on going down the wrong path. Peter was bitter, you remember, but only because he had not yet experienced first-hand Christ's amazing willingness to love, forgive, and renew him. Peter's problem was not that Christ had not forgiven him, but that he had not forgiven himself. Three times Jesus asked him, *"Do you love Me?"*[3]

Three times Peter tried his best to answer the question but his best was not good enough. It was the loving Lord's way of making

Peter face his own inadequacy and Christ's all sufficient grace. He was demonstrating that Peter's love might at times be fickle but His own love for Peter would always be invariable.

Today God comes to us with the same question. He is not oblivious to our sins. His eye has followed us into each wayward wandering. He is a first-person witness to the change it brought over us and in us by each of life's experiences, good or bad. We have changed but He has not. He still asks: *"Do you love Me?"* No matter what our answer, He still loves us with the same amazing love He alone can give. Our sins can no more change His heart toward us than Roman nails could keep Him on a cross.

His message is still, *"Behold! I stand at the door and knock. If anyone hears my voice and opens the door, I will come in and eat with him, and he with me."*[4] Today His knock is constant. The only inconstant is how we shall answer. He never changes.

Therefore, He alone must be the Cornerstone of the church as we minister in this new day. He is the unchanging One. That is a principle we can build our lives on. It is unwavering, resolute, unchanging, and non-negotiable. There will never be a day in this world or in the next when Jesus Christ is not the Lord of all things. He was Lord at creation. He was Lord when my grandparents' grandparents' grandparents were alive. He will be Lord when my grandchildren's grandchildren's grandchildren are alive.

Our Unfailing Lord

"Jesus Christ is the same yesterday and today and forever." Other religious systems, philosophies, and life itself will change and pass—

likely at an increasingly faster pace. But Christ always remains the same. The splendid Gothic building, commonly called First Presbyterian Church of Pittsburgh, changes. As a matter of fact, it is the fourth First Church building in Pittsburgh. The first three buildings stood at different locations. The first was a log cabin church built to bear witness to Jesus Christ and meet the needs of the earliest congregation. The second and larger building, constructed of red bricks, was designed to meet the ministry needs of a growing congregation and city. The third was built with gray stone and was larger than the second. All three of those buildings stood facing Wood Street around the corner from where the church now stands. A study of old Pittsburgh photographs at the Sen. John Heinz History Center quickly demonstrates that the city has always been a place of transition. A church with the city in its heart must change to meet the changing needs of its environment. As the city and its buildings have changed, the church edifice has changed with them. The address is different but our Lord is always the same, *"Yesterday and today and forever."* In Francis Shaeffer's words, "He is always there."

One of the ways God demonstrates His continuing love for us is by sending new disciples with an expanding array of talents to serve Christ among us. Just as buildings have changed, so also the faces in our church pews and figures in our pulpits and Sunday School classrooms have changed. Little children have been baptized, grown to adulthood, and been married. Some have graduated from among us to the Church Triumphant. New programs have been introduced, while old ones have died or been revitalized to meet changing needs. But the Lord of Christ's Church is constant. He is the only member no longer subject to death. He has been our Captain. He still is. He will be. This is our pledge to Him and to one another, and so we should make it our cornerstone.

He unites seed and egg to form our children at conception and wakes them to life on Earth at birth. He seals them to Himself in baptism, and saves them to Himself in conversion. He nurtures them to Himself through sanctification, restores them to Himself when they fail, and raises them to Himself when they are knocked down. He feeds us, warms us, and loves us until that day when the last of us join the first of us on that shore where there is no sunset and no shadow.

When we are slow to act, Christ is slow to anger. When we look dirty with sin, He sees past the dirt to our potential and washes us clean with His blood shed once for all on Calvary. No day will ever come for us—not tomorrow, not this year, not next year, indeed, not ever—when we will wake up without His love. There is no grave side where He is not present and no burden too big for His shoulders to bear.

All He Was, He Is; All He Is, He Will Be Forever!

This Jesus who never changes is in the business of transforming lives. His miracle-working power still transforms people for the better today. This is why we exist in His name. Do you know Him as your personal Lord and Savior? I hope so. If you do not, I ask you to invite Him into your heart now. Simply pray quietly where you are as you read this, "Lord Jesus Christ, I ask you to forgive my sins and I invite you into my life from this day forward. All I am and have are yours now and forever. Amen."

When we pray that prayer, or one like it, Christ comes into our lives and begins to transform us into better people. Receive Him today and you will never again be alone or grope in the dark for life's meaning. Seek not a guide, a leader, or a husband for your soul. You have the Lord of eternity within your heart. All He ever was, He is; and all He is, He always will be. He is our Cornerstone, the bedrock belief of who we are, and the first pillar on which we build this Mission Statement: *"Jesus Christ is the same yesterday and today and forever."* That will never change!

Our Foundation:
The Bible, God's Word

Isaiah 40:8
*"The grass withers and the flowers fall, but
the word of our God stands forever."*

❧～✦

2 Timothy 3:16–17
*"All Scripture is God-breathed and is useful
for teaching, rebuking, correcting and training
in righteousness, so that the man of God may
be thoroughly equipped for every good work."*

❧～✦

In His great High Priestly Prayer on the night before His trial and crucifixion, Jesus prays for us to be *"sanctified by the truth"* then adds these words, *"Your word is truth."*⁵ This is our Lord's final great affirmation that God's word has the power to change our lives for the better but that it too, like our cornerstone, never changes. This Mission Statement begins by laying a cornerstone saying that *"Jesus Christ is the same yesterday and today and forever."* Following that, the first firm declaration is that the Bible, God's Word, is the foundation on which our lives stand.

> *"We stand steadfastly for our foundation...*
> *the Bible, God's Word."*

Here is the second great, unchanging, irreducible truth on which this mission statement is founded. The Bible is the Word of God. What do we mean by that? We mean that we hold the Bible to be God's infallible, inerrant Word and the foundation for everything we do and try to be. Why? Because the Bible is eternally true. *"The word of our God stands forever,"* Isaiah says. It cannot be changed. The Bible alone shall be the book of our pulpit, our Sunday School, and the various arms of ministry in which our church is involved for Christ's sake. This belief in the high authority of Scripture is a distinctive that will set us apart from many other fellowships or congregations. We live, as was written in the last chapter, in a world of theological relativism. Theological relativism, often called "The New Age," puts its emphasis on excessive individuality. It says that our first goal is to be true to ourselves.

Translated into the vernacular of our day theological relativism declares that the Bible is only true if I decide it is true for me. Similarly, only that part is true which I have decided is true for me. Therefore, according to this way of thinking, if I believe that some parts of the Bible are true and some parts are not true, that is all right.

I believe, however, that truth is true no matter who speaks it and who does or does not believe it. Truth does not depend on popular acceptance to be true. Truth is absolute. It stands alone.

When we declare the Bible to be God's infallible and inerrant Word, and true in all its parts, that declaration at once leads us to what philosophy calls the epistemological question.

Epistemology is that division of philosophy and learning that investigates the nature and origin of knowledge. How do we know what we know? How do you know, for example, that two plus two equals four? How do we know that the Bible is God's inspired Word? A well-produced, current television commercial sets the Book of Mormon on a par with the Bible. How do we know that the Bible is the Word of God and the Book of Mormon is not?

THE TESTIMONY OF THE BIBLE

We know first of all because the Bible unequivocally and repeatedly claims to be God's revealed word and no credible witness has ever successfully refuted that claim. Most of the scriptures of the other great religions never make such a claim for themselves. Buddha, for example, never claims that his writings are divine revelation, neither does Confucius. In contrast, more than two thousand times the Old Testament alone claims: *"This is what the Lord said," "The word of the Lord came to,"* and *"God said."* How do we know that the Bible is God's unique word? The Bible self-attests that it is God's Word and when it makes such a declaration it puts its own credibility on the line.

Not only do Old Testament writers say God's word is inspired, but New Testament authors also testify to biblical inspiration. No one person is any more determined to make this point than the apostle Paul who tells young preacher Timothy, *"All Scripture is God-breathed."*

In doing so, Paul first makes a sturdy assertion. Secondly, he coins a powerful new Greek word. His assertion comes in the form of the word, all. The word Paul uses means there are no exceptions to the statement he is about to make. His new word is actually a compound of two Greek words. The word is *theopneustos*, from *Theos* for God, plus *pneustos* (from which we get our word *pneumatic*) for breath. In a sense, Paul is not only saying that God inspired the Scriptures but that He actually breathed them out through the hands of human authors. That is to say that the Holy Spirit allowed the writers to use their own styles, personalities, and figures of speech while sealing the accuracy of the message they wrote. So we conclude that the Bible is God's Word given through chosen, guarded personalities for us because the book itself says so.

The Testimony of the Prophets

After the testimony of the Bible itself there is also the testimony of the prophets, who wrote in advance of events actually happening. Whole books are written on this subject. Think about just a few Bible prophecies concerning the birth of Jesus.

More than seven hundred years before Christ was born, the prophet Isaiah said that John the Baptizer would be Christ's forerunner and that Jesus would be born of a virgin mother.[6] About the same time, the prophet Micah testified with incredible accuracy that Jesus would be born in a tiny hamlet called Bethlehem.[7] The book of Psalms, written between approximately 1440 and 586 years before Jesus was born, is filled with prophecies about His life, death, and message. Psalm 22, for example, predicted He would die on a cross and that evil men would cast lots for

His clothes, and Psalm 16:8–10 says He would rise again from the dead. The stunning accuracy with which these and many other prophecies speak about our Savior hundreds of years before He was born stand as proof positive that He is truly the Messiah of God and that no ordinary hand guided the pen that wrote the book we call the Holy Bible.

Consider against this that the only prophecy in the Koran, Islam's holy book, is one Mohammed proposed to control himself: He said that he would return to Mecca. Jesus, Lord of the cross, on the other hand, prophesied He would return from the dead, and He did!

Bible prophecies are not, of course, restricted to Christ alone or even to people. There are amazing prophecies about places. Take, for example, the City of Nineveh, capital of the historic Assyrian Empire. Nineveh ruled the world of its day. When Nineveh was at its peak, Nahum prophesied, *"The LORD has given a command concerning you, Nineveh: 'You will have no descendants to bear your name. I will destroy the carved images and cast idols that are in the temple of your gods. I will prepare your grave, for you are vile.'"*[8]

Nineveh's egotistical pagan scholars laughed in Nahum's face. They foolishly believed that Nineveh was indestructible. What happened? Edward Gibbon, writing in *The Rise and Fall of the Roman Empire,* describes the destruction of Nineveh in ways that parallel Nahum's words completely. This is perhaps especially remarkable inasmuch as Edward Gibbon was a self-professing skeptic when it came to religion.

After Nineveh fell from prominence Babylon, modern Baghdad, rose to power. Babylon was probably the greatest city ever built.

Totally self-sufficient, Babylon had a balance of trade unequaled in history. Babylon needed to import nothing. It was the kind of situation politicians and economists dream about.

Babylon's citizens were intelligent. Long before there was an English language, Babylonians saw the need for writing down language in a universal way and gave civilization the first-ever alphabetized language.

Do modern computers impress you? They do me. Babylonian scholars developed the base-10 system of mathematics on which our mathematical system is founded. Had Babylonians not given us that foundation, computers might never have been developed. Look at the time on your watch. Babylonians first saw the value of measuring time and invented the first clocks and calendars to measure it.

As I write these words during my summer vacation, I can look out of a window across from my desk and survey San Francisco's fascinating skyline. Not far away is the world famous Transamerica Building with its lofty, pointed tower reaching toward the heavens. From what I have observed, it seems that every one of these buildings is finished in concrete. Babylonians first saw the value of baking clay into concrete blocks for construction purposes. Before Babylon rose to prominence, builders in other societies regarded clay as nothing more than muck. They considered it useless as a building material except for the most temporary of buildings. The Babylonians were the first great students of science. Today almost every branch of the scientific world can trace its roots to ancient Babylon.

We have all seen television photographs of China's Great Wall. The Babylonians constructed a larger, stronger, and more impenetrable wall than China's wall thousands of years before Chinese architects drew up their plans. It was as wide as some parts of the American interstate highway system, designed so that four chariots could be driven side-by-side around its perimeter. The Babylonians were very proud of it. By way of intimidating contrast, Babylon scorned Jerusalem's walls as tiny by comparison and threatened to break down the walls and crush Jerusalem. Isaiah, in turn, called Babylon *"the jewel of kingdoms,"*[9] and forecast a Babylonian doom equal to Sodom and Gomorrah if Babylon ever attempted to carry out that threat. The brilliant Babylonian warlords mocked him, saying Isaiah was a nobody. They sneered about him being deluded. Ego convinced them they would be the leading city of the world for all time. But, *"those who walk in pride God is able to humble."*[10] In God's perfect timing, Isaiah's words came true and Babylon's walls fell.

Jerusalem's city walls, on the other hand, still stand. I have walked across them. God, through Isaiah,[11] Jeremiah,[12] Daniel,[13] and Micah[14] foretold Babylon's future of troublesome times and tyrannical leaders. What is happening in Babylon today? Saddam Hussein, "the Butcher of Baghdad," has been toppled from his throne as the latest in a line of despots. That should not surprise us. God's Word said it would be so.

THE TESTIMONY OF THE LORD

Our Lord Jesus Christ was committed to the authority of the Scriptures. *"It is written,"*[15] He replied every time Satan tempted

Him. For the Lord, what the Scriptures said was enough and settled a matter conclusively. When the religious leaders of His day challenged Him, He pointed out that they were failing to understand their own holy writings. *"You diligently study the Scriptures because you think that by them you possess eternal life. These are the Scriptures that testify about me, yet you refuse to come to me to have life."*[6] That Christ held the Scriptures to be trustworthy and recognized their authority is an absolute and undeniable fact. That alone should sufficiently inspire all who claim to be His disciples to study His Word.

Yet, the Scriptures tell us even more about the Lord Jesus than that He had confidence in them. They also demonstrate how far He was willing to go to redeem us. You can search the world over and read every book ever written, but you will never find another book like the one that first told humanity about God's love in Jesus.

GOD'S INCREDIBLE BOOK

Think about it. Here is a book written by assorted writers from unrelated backgrounds who speak various languages with diverse dialects. They include a king, a physician, a herdsman, a tax collector, a theologian, a scribe, and a fisherman. In a time before the Internet and fax, when communication was virtually non-existent, it is very likely many of them had no idea the others even existed. In such diversity there was not much hope for collusion or communication. Forty different writers spread over sixty-four generations produced sixty-eight books with the complete harmony and precision of a well-made jigsaw puzzle. Together they tell us everything we need to know about God who made all things. They promise that God will meet us in our every need and heal our every hurt. They inspire us in our lowliness, accompany us in our loneliness, strengthen us in our weakness, and bring us through our dark nights into bright new tomorrows. There is a positive word of encouragement for every decision we shall ever face. Above all else, this book speaks plainly about God's love for us in Jesus, His Son, who died on a Roman cross and rose again. It has no equal. How else would we explain this book except to say that it comes to us by the hand of God?

So, this Mission Statement declares for all the world to see that we are a people of one book and our book is the Bible, the Word of God written for us. God's great book is about Jesus meeting you and me at the point of our deepest need. This book is our foundation because we all need a foundation on which to build our lives together.

You also need a firm foundation on which to build a life worth living or a business worth developing. Thus God gives the Bible as the book of His life for you. Take it up. Read it and, in God's power, live it.

Our Lord: Jesus Christ, God's Only Son

Colossians 1:19
*"God was pleased to have all his fullness
dwell in him, and through him to recon-
cile to himself all things, whether things on
earth or things in heaven, by making peace
through his blood, shed on the cross."*

Colossae, a multicultural city, was 125 miles southeast of Ephesus on the way to Rome. The population was principally
composed of immigrants from Greece, Rome, and Israel. As far
as we know, the apostle Paul never visited there. However, his influence was felt among the Christians in Colossae because of stories travelers to Colossae told about Paul's ministry in Ephesus.

When Billy Graham preached at Three Rivers Stadium in Pittsburgh, my parents, who were visiting from Ireland attended the
meetings. Later they traveled on to Waterloo, Ontario, Canada,

where they spent time with my sister, Sandra, and her family. The next time I was in Waterloo, a friend of my sister's spoke about Billy Graham's meetings in Pittsburgh—based on my parents' report. Paul's relationship with the Colossian Christians was in a similar vein. People who sat under Paul's preaching talked about it wherever their journeys took them. He was a speaker with a good reputation and his message was one worth repeating.

Therefore, when confusion arose in the Colossian church it was no surprise that Epaphras, a Colossian Christian who perhaps had business in Rome, visited Paul in prison there. Epaphras told Paul about new teachings that threatened the purity of the gospel in the Colossian church. He asked for Paul's advice. In that context one of the great epistles of the New Testament was born and included in it was the most succinct definition of the person of Christ in the entire Bible. *"God was pleased to have all his fullness dwell in him."*

The defective new teaching that was infecting the Colossian church—like a deadly virus of the soul—was called Gnosticism. Gnosticism reckoned Christianity to be a purely academic matter. Setting knowledge on a higher level of importance than a personal relationship with Christ, it even called into question who Jesus was. Compounding that confusion was Gnosticism's stipulation that the old Jewish temple rites and traditions must still be followed for salvation to be complete. Thus, Gnostic teachers promoted circumcision, dietary laws, and the Jewish feast observances as necessary parts of salvation. In their failure to see that Christ alone is all we need to be saved, they missed the essence of Christian faith.

They are not alone in their confused understanding. As strange a doctrine as it seems at first glance, it recurs in almost every generation in church history. Today it is the core of Jehovah's Witness teaching. It presents a destructive and unhealthy view of the gospel that challenges Christ's deity by saying He is not God, but the highest of all created beings, a creature rather than the Creator. Paul's primary purpose in writing his Colossian letter is to refute this notion. *"God was pleased to have all his fullness dwell in him."*

These words are the Bible text for the second pillar of the Mission Statement:

> *We stand steadfastly for:*
> *Our Foundation . . . the Bible, God's Word;*
> *Our Lord . . . Jesus Christ, God's only Son.*

How do we know that Jesus Christ, God's Son, is Lord?

WE KNOW BECAUSE HE TELLS US

Throughout His sermons and teachings Jesus repeatedly claims attributes and powers that are God's alone. He asserts His pre-existence: *"Before Abraham was born, I am!"*[17] He declares His omnipotence: *"All authority in heaven and on earth has been given to me."*[18] He says He is infallible: *"Heaven and earth will pass away, but my words will never pass away."*[19] He promises His omnipresence: *"I am with you always."*[20] He maintains personal moral perfection: *"Can any of you prove me guilty of sin?"*[21] He advances His right to judge: *"The Father judges no one, but has entrusted all judgment to the Son."*[22] He professes His power to forgive sins: *"Friend, your sins are forgiven."*[23] Finally, in an act which if at all untrue would be absolute blasphemy, He asserts total equality with God: *"I and the Father are one."*[24] In all these ways, and many more, Jesus Christ claimed to be God. In one of the most pointed declarations of all literature, Christ even went so far as to declare that He alone was the way to God. *"I am the way and the truth and the life. No one comes to the Father except through me."*[25]

Lunatic? Liar? Lord!

To paraphrase another son of Belfast, C. S. Lewis, when Christ makes these claims for Himself there are finally only three possible conclusions we can draw. The first is that He was deluded by visions of grandeur. If that is the case we must declare Him a lunatic. The second is that He was perpetrating what has become the greatest confidence scheme ever carried out in human history, in which case let us declare Him a liar without equal. The third is that He is indeed everything He claims to be and we must surrender our lives completely to Him.

Three Great Miracles

Furthermore, we know that Jesus is Lord because of three great miracles Scripture connects to His life. First, He was born of a virgin just as the prophet Isaiah said He would be. *"The Lord himself will give you a sign: The virgin will be with child and will give birth to a son"*[26] and as Matthew also confirms.[27] Second, He was resurrected from the dead, just as the psalmist David declared and as Luke the physician and gospel writer reported He would be.[29] *"I have set the LORD always before me. Because he is at my right hand, I will not be shaken. Therefore my heart is glad and my tongue rejoices; my body also will rest secure, because you will not abandon me to the grave, nor will you let your Holy One see decay.*"[28] Third, He ascended into heaven just as was David foretold. *"When you ascended on high, you led captives in your train; you received gifts from men, even from the re-bellious—that you, O LORD God, might dwell there,*"[30] as Paul tells us in his Ephesian letter.[31]

THE INTEGRITY OF HIS TEACHINGS

We also know that Jesus is Lord because of the integrity of His teachings. In almost two thousand years, no one has improved on even one of His ethical principles, and no teaching of His has become obsolete. John Stuart Mill, the nineteenth-century philosopher and scholar, asked, "Who among the disciples or their proselytes was capable of inventing the sayings ascribed to Jesus, or imagining the life and character revealed in the Gospel? Certainly not the fishermen of Galilee; and certainly not St. Paul! Still less the early Christian writers, in whom nothing was more evident than that the good that was in them was all derived, as they always confessed, from Him."[32]

THE CHARACTER QUESTION

One of the most chilling concerns about recent national elections in America is the strong indicator of moral ambivalence revealed about us. Polling data indicates the American public no longer considers character a primary concern for persons in leadership. We seem to be saying that we believe we can expect good leadership from bad people, or that people with questionable lifestyles can provide a certain positive moral example worth following. We are in what Stephen Vincent Benet calls, "A time with few fixed stars."[33]

Yet, the Bible teaches and history confirms that character means everything in leadership. Just as the old mariners once charted their courses across the oceans by studying the stars, so even now every life needs "a few fixed stars." That is, we all need something or someone by whom we can set our moral compass. We need life foundations that will not erode in a temporal, fleeting, stressful, and uncertain world. No other system of belief in all history stands or falls with the character of its founder like Christianity. Christianity is, after all, not about a system of doctrine but about the person called Jesus Christ, the God-Man. Discredit Him in just one point and suddenly Christianity is no more.

If someone successfully disproved any one thing Jesus Christ said or took credit for doing—even one—two thousand years of Christian glory would lie in ruins and every disciple of Jesus would be discredited to the extent he or she professed Christ's Lordship.

For two thousand years people have dedicated their lives to undermining the good character and moral honor of Jesus Christ. They have included people from almost every scholarly discipline imaginable, yet none has ever succeeded in finding a flaw. Dr. Clarence Edward Macartney, in a published sermon titled, "God the Son," writes, "The very charges which his enemies brought against him were tributes to his character."

This statement is true. Every time Jesus Christ's enemies charged Him with something, it was a half-truth which, when the whole truth was told, served not only to vindicate Him but to elevate Him. His enemies said He was a Sabbath-breaker, but an investigation of the charge proves that by healing on the Sabbath

He put the day in the context God intended. Other adversaries called Him a winebibber, but when the charge was pursued He was shown to demonstrate hands-on concern for society's down and outs. Other opponents charged that He was in league with the Devil, but a closer look at His life and at the gospel He left us proves that He broke, and is still breaking, Satan's power over people. When He rose up from the grave, He broke Satan's grip on death and made the last enemy a graduation exercise into an eternal place of unequaled glory.

All of these tell us something about who Christ is. Our text challenges us to consider also what Christ has done. During His life on earth and in the two thousands years since He established His church, more people have been educated, healed, positively redirected, and inspired in His name than in all the other names in the history of the world. Only in His name do we find the forgiveness of sins guaranteed.

Our Advocate

The online edition of my hometown newspaper, the Belfast Telegraph, recently reported a story about a lawyer whose car was stolen. The next day he received a call from a former client asking for defense against a charge of car theft. Upon further inquiry, the lawyer discovered that the car in question was his car. Through a strange turn of events, the victim was hired to defend the thief. When that representation of that client by that attorney was challenged in court, the lawyer responded his client admitted guilt. It was, therefore, perfectly appropriate for him to advocate on behalf of his client, he argued.

Let me tell you what the Bible says about Jesus. *"My dear children, I write this to you so that you will not sin. But if anybody does sin, we have one who speaks to the Father in our defense—Jesus Christ, the Righteous One. He is the atoning sacrifice for our sins, and not only for ours but also for the sins of the whole world."*[34]

John reaches into the language of the legal world of his day and finds a word declaring that Jesus does more than represent us as our attorney when we do wrong against Him. The good the attorney might do for that accused thief is limited. This Jesus who represents us, actually offers Himself to pay our penalty. No attorney I ever heard of ever served his client's sentence. Yet, that is precisely what Jesus Christ did for us. He is, therefore, not only our advocate but our propitiate. He took our sin and its punishment upon Himself at Calvary's cross, just as Isaiah prophesied He would: *"He was pierced for our transgressions, he was crushed for our iniquities; the punishment that brought us peace was upon him, and by his wounds we are healed."*[35]

Consider this: Christ Jesus, the One offended by all our sins, not only rushes to our defense, He personally bears the penalty our sins deserve. In so doing, He sets us free from having to suffer it. Amazing as that may seem, it is all the more wondrous that He does all this pro bono, or at no expense to us. What a gracious, generous Lord! The eternal life He offers us costs us nothing even though it cost Him life itself.

THE FULLNESS FOUND IN CHRIST ALONE

"For God was pleased to have all his fullness dwell in him." Everything that God is and wants us to be is found in His Son Jesus Christ, the perfect God-man. Jesus is truly God to the fullest extent possible. Nothing

God has is lacking in Him. When it comes to humanity, He is the only perfect person who ever lived. The only one who did not need a Savior became the Savior of the world.

All God's fullness found in Christ radiates toward us. Everything you want God to be is found in God's Son, Jesus. John Wesley says it powerfully in his great hymn:

Thou, O Christ, art all I want; more than all in Thee I find.

What This Means For Us

What does this mean for us? It means that because Jesus is all the fullness of God we have a great Redeemer from sin, One whose blood makes us clean. It means we have a firm foundation on which to build a life of faith. It means that, with Paul, we *"live by faith in the Son of God who loved us and gave Himself for us."*[36] This brings me at last to personalize this pillar from the Mission Statement, for this church is, finally, you.

Christ has no hands but ours to do His work. He has no feet but ours to take His ministry to the needy and less blessed people of our generation. He has no lips but ours to tell the lost the way to eternal life with Him in His Father's house of many mansions.

Is Jesus Christ your Lord? If your answer is in the affirmative that begs this question: What will you give your life to in His service? How will you demonstrate Christ's presence in your life? Christ has high expectations for His people in every church that bears His name. He has exciting dreams for you no matter what your life's calling. Each of us is gifted in unique ways for His service.

Christ's Reveille trumpet is sounding in your heart as you read these words. Do you hear it? Are you listening?

THEMES TO THINK ON - THINGS TO DO

1. Before they can become the unchangeable principles of
your organization, the same principles must be the principles that undergird your personal life. What principles
are non-negotiables in your life?

2. Write them out using five words or less for each one.
Place them where you will see them often.

3. Now write out some ways they have made a difference
so far and how you can imagine them holding you firm for
the future.

Priorities We Stand For

Irreducible but Adjustable Commitments We Intend to Keep

Our Highest Priority:
To Proclaim Christ's Cross

1 Corinthians 1:17-18
*"The message of the cross is foolishness to
those who are perishing, but to us who are
being saved it is the power of God."*

Not only are there unchanging principles that we stand on,
there are also priorities that we stand for. These are the
irreducible commitments we make to God and to one another.
They may be adjustable in terms of which one is the priority at
any given moment but that does not change the fact that they are
still irreducible reasons for our existence. In this chapter and the
four chapters that follow in this section, we will explore some of
these priorities and the reasons for them.

Crosses, according to an article in Vogue magazine not long ago,
are back in style. The high-fashion world is promoting a popular
revival of cross sales in jewelry stores and fashion boutiques all

across America. Crosses have become a definitive fashion accessory of the moment for both men and women. You have no doubt seen them, worn around necks, as earrings or pinned to jacket lapels by people who are style conscious. Some crosses look very attractive and give evidence of great creativity. I even saw one worn as a finger ring a few days ago. Perhaps you wear one yourself either as a fashion statement or a faith statement.

The Sign of the Cross

A member of the congregation stopped by the office to ask if we had a color photograph of the Covenanter church flag. She was planning to participate in a historical reenactment of the earliest days of our country and wanted to accurately replicate the flag colors. The Covenanters are noted for their unique commitment level and certain practices that set them apart from other Christians. For example, the Covenanters until recently sang all their songs only from the Psalms and always without musical instruments.

Almost every religious system or philosophical ideology in world history has identified itself through the use of some flag or symbol. Ancient Buddhism's lotus flower, for example, depicted the emergence of beauty from the muddy waters of chaos, while Islam's crescent symbolizes the Muslim conquest of the Old World and intention to capture the New World to its cause. Marxism's hammer and sickle, no longer as popular as it once was, represents the convergence of industry and agriculture through the Industrial Revolution.

Do you know why Hitler's forces lost the Second World War? It was because the Third Reich's intention was to replace the

Christian cross with the Swastika, which some people think of as a cross of distorted shape. Adolf Hitler planned for all of Europe's churches to submit to his personal control and direction much as the Communists did in Eastern Europe until not long ago. Point 30 of the National Reich Church Program expressed the intention to replace the Christian cross with the Swastika in every church sanctuary in Europe: "On the day of (the Reich's) foundation, the Christian cross must be removed from all churches, cathedrals and chapels," Nazi leaders wrote. "It must be superseded by the only unconquerable symbol, the Swastika." No wonder the Third Reich lost the war! They unwittingly plotted their own destruction when they wrote those words. They thought the cross foolish, but it is the power of God. History is a commentary on the folly of those who think that somehow they can replace such a primary symbol of Christian faith with a self-serving substitute. Jesus said, *"I will build my church, and the gates of Hades will not overcome it."*[37]

Ancient Judaism rejected visual symbols of its religion out of respect for the second commandment: *"You shall not make for yourself an idol in the form of anything in heaven above or on the earth beneath or in the waters below."*[38] On a recent trip to Israel, however, it was obvious that modern Israeli leaders have relaxed that rule for we saw the Star of David at the center of Israel's national flag hanging from public buildings in every town and freely available on jewelry and in clothing designs.

In the eighth century a hearty dispute, based on the same logic as the rule of old Israel, raged over all Christendom. Historians call it the Iconoclastic Controversy. One side said church buildings should bear no symbols lest the symbols themselves become objects of worship. The opposing side argued for a proliferation of symbols, saying they would help the people recall the history and primary elements of Christian faith. Within the body of Christ today, many still hold strong views on this subject.

Long before the Iconoclastic Controversy, earlier Christians avoided being identified with the cross for fear of being cruelly persecuted. For the first generation of believers, wearing a cross was looking for trouble. The cross was too readily recognized by those who opposed the gospel. Therefore, for the early disciples the cherished and most widely recognized insignia was not a cross but a fish. The fish became a nearly universal Christian sign and for good reason. The Greek word for fish, *icthus*, served as an acronym for *Iesus Christos, Theou, Huios, Soterios*,—"Jesus Christ, God, Son, Savior!" That was, in a sense, the first creed of Christ's followers. Not until the second century did the cross replace the fish as the principal symbol of the gospel of Jesus Christ. So we rejoice when persons of every religious persuasion, or of no religion, wear a cross for, whether they realize it or not, they bear witness to the price that was paid to redeem us. Moreover, when the cross is empty it implicitly testifies to Christ's resurrection.

THE FOOLISH CROSS

"The message of the cross is foolishness to those who are perishing," Paul writes to the Corinthians. Marcus Tullius Cicero, that forceful orator who lived a century before Christ and whose eloquence moved the Roman Senate and whose rational leadership skills helped elevate him among his peers to the highest office in the Roman Republic, said, "The cross speaks of that which is so shameful, so horrible, it should never be mentioned in polite so-

ciety." He should have known, for it was he who led the Roman Senate to adopt the cross as the most heinous way imaginable to demonstrate Rome's power over its subjects.

The cross does not, however, find its roots in Rome. In ancient Egypt the cross was already a well-known symbol before Rome rose to power. There it was called a *canob*, after a T-shaped instrument used to measure the rise and fall of the Nile. The same is true in Greece. As early as 125 BC, worshippers of the Greek god Bacchus presented him with flour cakes having the figure of a cross imprinted on them. When Rome rose to prominence as the world's leading power, however, the cruel practice of nailing society's worst criminals to a cross in a public place was adopted not only for punishment but also as a deterrent against crime.

The cross was the electric chair of its time. It said a person was unfit to live; rejected by humanity, and accursed of God. The cross declared that the one hanging on it was not worthy of a place in decent society.

The Ultimate Plus Sign

The apostle Paul, a citizen of Rome, knew all this from his study of history. After his dramatic conversion on the Damascus Road, however, he became more broad-minded than Cicero. Paul saw what God had done with Rome's most horrible symbol and wrote, *"May I never boast except in the cross of our Lord Jesus Christ, through which the world has been crucified to me, and I to the world."*[39]

Cicero, had he lived to see it, would have called Christ's death on the cross an unsurpassed shame. Paul, the well-educated son of Roman aristocracy who once would have agreed with Cicero, came to regard the cross of Jesus as the only thing he knew worth bragging about. The cross was indeed rough and deadly, but it was, above all else, effective in accomplishing God's plan for our redemption. That it is worn with pride by leaders in high fashion is wonderful testimony to the way God can take a thing of abject disgrace and transform it into something of beauty and splendor. God made the ugly cross of the Romans the world's ultimate plus sign.

It is no wonder then that John Bunyan in his immortal *Pilgrim's Progress* says, "I saw in my dream that just as Christian came up to the cross, his burden loosed from his shoulders and fell from his back and began to tumble till it came to the mouth of the sepulcher, where it fell and I saw it no more. Then was Christian glad and lightsome and said with a merry heart, 'He has given me rest by his sorrow, and life by his death.'" Let his words bring life to every Christian.

Dress it up however you like, but it finally comes down to this: Your heart and mine were so putrid in the sight of the holy God that there was no other possible way by which we might be saved. We needed a cross. God took this instrument the world once looked upon with disdain and, through the death of His Son, turned it into an instrument of glory for us.

ALREADY DEAD

It is unfortunate that the translators opted for the word "perishing" in our Scripture text. *"For the message of the cross is foolishness to those who are perishing."* The original word carries more force than that. It really means abject lostness so that a more accurate translation might read, "The message of the cross is foolishness to lost people." The point is that there is a finality about rejecting the cross.

Do you see the difference? Let me illustrate it another way. Paul does not say we are in the process of perishing, that we are on the way to being lost, or that we will be lost if we persist in rejecting Christ's cross. He says that outside this cross of Jesus Christ we are already dead and already lost. It is the difference between a journey and a destination. That is why repentance is a necessary part of Christian conversion for it requires a backing up, as it were.

The preeminent Scottish poet-preacher, George MacLeod, writes:

> "I simply argue that the cross be raised again at the center of the market place as well as on the steeple of the church. I am recovering the claim that Jesus was not crucified in a cathedral between two candles; but on a cross between two thieves on a town garbage heap; at a crossroad of politics so cosmopolitan that they had to write His title in Hebrew and in Latin and in Greek . . . . And at the kind of place where cynics talk smut, and thieves curse and soldiers gamble. Because that is where He died, and that is what He died about. And that is where Christ's men ought to be, and what church people ought to be about."

So we preach the message of the cross with a high degree of urgency. It is the focal point of the Mission Statement we've been examining:

We stand steadfastly for:
Our Foundation... the Bible, God's Word;
Our Lord... Jesus Christ, God's only Son;
Our highest priority... to proclaim Christ's cross

In making a statement such as this we recognize that the pseudo-sophistication of our society will cause some people who hear our message of the cross to reject it. We always regret their decision. Some will call us out of touch with our day. This we accept, knowing that we live in an age that often seems to prefer to speak only of God's love and chooses not to remember the desperate final pain God's Son endured on the cross to demonstrate the length to which God's love was willing to go for our sake. We also prefer to speak about God's love, but we know that there can be no Easter without Calvary, for the cross always precedes the resurrection. When others oppose our message we respectfully but simply revert to Paul's inspired words. *"The message of the cross is foolishness to those who are lost . . . God was pleased through the foolishness of what was preached to save those who believe."*[40]

The cross at Calvary exposes sin in all its wretchedness and the utter worthlessness of all human efforts at redemption. The cross demonstrates the price God places on a human soul. In the cross we find our life and our reason for being. In the cross we find our health and our hope for all eternity. In the cross we find our victories and our protection from our enemies. No powers that earth can imagine could ever separate us from God's love in Christ crucified.

GRANNY WAS DEAD WRONG!
An elderly Scots woman went to church regularly most of her life. She always hoped that when she died she would get dying

grace and be fit for heaven. One night two preachers spoke at the same service. Walking home she met an inquisitive neighbor who asked, "How was church, Granny?"

"We had two preachers tonight," said she.

"Did you like them?"

"No. I couldn't understand them. One said he was preaching to folk already saved. The people he described were so good I couldn't think of a single soul in our village like that. The other said he was here to speak to people that are lost. He said they are going to hell."

"Which of the two did you prefer?" the neighbor inquired further.

"Neither one," said Granny. "Can you imagine that they had two preachers and neither one had a word for me?"

"Neither one had a word for me." According to Granny's estimation, she was neither lost nor found. That, however, is not a realistic option. The cross, once a symbol of death, is now a symbol of life and hope, and for the church in the new millennium, the only symbol that guarantees life for sinners. Yet, the fact remains that the Bible says there are just two kinds of people in all the world. There are those people who are lost because they reject the message of the cross and those people who are saved because they put full trust in the Christ of Calvary's cross.

As you read this you are either a lost person right now, or a saved person right now. Which are you? You must be one or the other.

Granny was wrong. There was a word for her that evening. Any time the gospel is preached there is always a word for each of us.

If you have never done so before, or if you once did but have somehow drifted away, why not commit or recommit your life to Christ Jesus as you come to the end of this chapter. Take for yourself the message of the cross and you can be sure Christ has saved you. When you receive Him into your life, come and join us or join another church where you can take part in lifting high the cross for Christ's sake.

Our Highest Priority: To Proclaim Christ's Resurrection

A fter the cross comes the resurrection. Therefore, the phrase we began to look at in chapter four does not end where we last left it. Instead, it quickly goes on to establish our commitment to Christ's overcoming death:

> *We stand steadfastly for:*
> *Our Foundation... the Bible, God's Word;*
> *Our Lord... Jesus Christ, God's only Son;*
> *Our highest priority...*
> *to proclaim Christ's cross and resurrection;*

CHRIST'S RESURRECTION

Auguste Comte, the French philosopher known as the Father of Sociology, was determined to start a new religion called Positivism. Comte believed that given enough time his new religion would supplant Christianity as the primary religion of Europe. With great enthusiasm Comte told his friend, the Scottish essayist and student of the French Revolution, Thomas Carlyle, of his plans. The sage Carlyle responded, "It sounds like an excellent idea, Comte. All you will need to do will be to speak as no man ever spoke before and live as none has ever been able to live. Next you must be crucified and rise again the third day. If you can do all this and get the world to believe that you are still alive and your being alive again really does inspire people to be better than they were, your new religion will last."

The Bible says that after His crucifixion Jesus' body was removed from the cross and buried in Joseph of Arimathea's garden tomb. Yet He is no longer there. The greatest miracle in all history occurred in that tomb. Christ rose again from the dead.

In the forty days following His resurrection, Christ appeared on no less than thirteen different occasions and to more than five hundred people. That was the central thrust that set the Christian Church in motion at its beginning. On the day of Pentecost it was the primary point of Peter's sermon when he proclaimed to thousands that *"God raised him from the dead, freeing him from the agony of death, because it was impossible for death to keep its hold on him."*[41]

THE RESURRECTION FACT

Peter's Pentecost sermon consisted of three undeniable points about Jesus' resurrection. There was a declaration, an affirmation, and an explanation. The declaration was that "God raised Him." This was followed by the affirmation that "It was impossible for death to keep its hold on Him." Finally, Peter explained that this was all part of God's eternal plan, quoting the prophetic words of Psalm 16. *"David said about him: I saw the Lord always before me. Because he is at my right hand, I will not be shaken. Therefore my heart is glad and my tongue rejoices; my body also will live in hope, because you will not abandon me to the grave, nor will you let your Holy One see decay. You have made known to me the paths of life; you will fill me with joy in your presence."*[42]

OUR RESURRECTION PROCLAMATION

When we say that we proclaim Christ's resurrection, we do not pretend we know all there is to know about it. We are willing learners in His service. With Paul the apostle, each of us declares, *"I want to know Christ and the power of his resurrection."*[43] Thus we aim to experience resurrection power personally every day in each of our lives and thereby to grow in the knowledge and love of the living Jesus.

Proclaiming Christ's resurrection sets us apart in four ways that affect all of life for us.

LIFE AFTER DEATH

First, it declares our belief in life after death. Jesus promised He would go to prepare a place for us, so that we would dwell with Him forever in His Father's house.

49

Second, death holds no eternal threat for us. We shall rise again, for He said so. *"I am the resurrection and the life. He who believes in me will live, even though he dies."*[44] *"Before long, the world will not see me anymore, but you will see me. Because I live, you also will live."*[45]

Only Christ's disciples can claim resurrection power for only Christ has conquered death. Think about it. Confucius' disciples, Buddha's disciples, and Mohammed's disciples find their masters' tombs occupied. I have visited Cairo, Egypt, and viewed the famous pyramids as our guide explained they were the burial places of ancient Egyptian kings and lingered at England's Westminster Abbey to read the cold stone slabs that mark the burial spot of some of England's great monarchs. Death has taken each of them away. However the tomb where Jesus, the King of Kings, once lay dead is vacant, for He has taken death away. Death died at Christ's tomb.

CHRIST'S DEITY

Third, our resurrection message tells the world we are committed to believe in Christ's deity. We confirm our conviction that all the prophecies and claims made about Him in the Bible are true. There is even more to our resurrection message than immortality. No ordinary mortal could rise from the dead. He who conquered death had to be the Son of the living God. Writing to the Romans Paul says Jesus was *"Declared with power to be the Son of God by his resurrection from the dead."*[46]

THE VICTORIOUS LIFE

Fourth, because we believe in a living Savior and because we believe that He is God, we believe in His power to bring victory over any situation or circumstance. "God raised him from the dead, freeing him from the agony of death, because it was impossible for death to keep its hold on him." Our resurrection message says our Christ declared victory over the grave: *"I am the Living One; I was dead, and behold I am alive for ever and ever!"*[47] If death could not hold Him, nothing can hold Him. If nothing can hold Him, we believe nothing can hold those who by grace belong to Him. We are the people of the resurrection. If it is really true that our Lord has conquered even death, the evidence of that truth needs to be seen in our everyday attitude and never more so than when tragedy strikes and trials try to take us down.

Four hundred years before Jesus lived, the Greek poet Agathon said, "Even God cannot change the past." Historically speaking, Agathon is right, of course. God never goes back and rewrites history nor does He call us to live yesterday again. The past is gone. Yet when God raised Christ from the dead, He provided a way to transform all our yesterdays into foundation stones for a wonderful new beginning. *"I will repay you for the years the locusts have eaten—the great locust and the young locust, the other locusts and the locust swarm."*[48]

LIFE OVER DEATH

We often hear talk about "the wasted years" of someone's life. God declares through Joel the prophet that He will make use even of our "wasted years."

There is something about the past in all of us that we wish was not there, but it is. What can we do about it? We can turn it over to God and He will find a way to redeem it in our new life in Him.

When we think back on how we have sometimes reacted in the face of pain, sorrow, ill-reproach, trouble, and temptation, we could hang our heads in shame. There are times in my own life when it must have looked as though the Lord I confessed was anemic and insufficient to meet my needs, unable to save Himself, much less me. Yet, the truth is that the weakness came at the point of my faith and not at the point of His power. Even Paul the apostle had to learn this. *"My grace is sufficient for you, for my power is made perfect in weakness."*[49] Is it not amazing that God takes the broken parts of our lives and makes us stronger because of them? No wonder Paul continued, *"Therefore I will boast all the more gladly about my weaknesses, so that Christ's power may rest on me."*

By restating the declaration of Christ's resurrection as part of our highest priority, we say His mighty power is available to transform lives today and make us more than conquerors. Therefore we give our weaknesses to Him and find new power to overcome them. Thus even these weaknesses become available for use toward God's glory. Christian history is replete with splendid examples of this. Here are but a few:

Consider Mary Magdalene. Who but Christ can take a woman of ill repute, broken by her illegitimate life style, scorned by her own people, and transform her into a fearless and godly daughter of God Almighty?

Consider Paul the apostle. Who but Christ could take a murder-ous, self-sufficient Pharisee and break him of his pride? In Christ he became the apostle to the Gentile world and a prolific writer to advance Christ's cause in every generation.

Consider John Newton, once a drunken slave trader so desperate for another drink that he sold himself into bondage. By God's grace he confronted the helplessness of his addiction to alcohol. Under Christ, John Newton was transformed into a powerful preacher, pastor, and hymn-writer who gave the world a hymn about his own life that is a Christian favorite because it tells the story of every believer's life:

> *Amazing grace, how sweet the sound*
> *That saved a wretch like me;*
> *I once was lost, but now am found;*
> *Was blind, but now I see.*

Consider Charles Colson. The articulate, tough-guy Marine vet-eran lawyer who proudly wore the title "Richard Nixon's hatch-et-man" was broken after a court convicted him for his part in crimes that shocked America. An encounter with God's grace in Jesus transformed him into a mighty evangelist to prisoners and apologist for the Christian faith in our generation.

Each of these people is a case study in what God through the resurrected Christ is able to do in any life. The resurrection mes-sage is not only that we have life over the death that is to come, but that we have life over the death in us that used to be. Christ alone can take the very worst things in our lives and orchestrate them for good and gain. In Him people who are spiritually dead are brought to life. This same resurrected Lord of the cross called Jesus of Nazareth is still at work in our world. He is able to take that which is dead and broken in any life and breathe new life into it for the gospel's sake. What sustains the church of Jesus Christ generation after generation is not that its people are perfect but that its Lord is both perfect and resurrected.

CHRIST'S RESURRECTION PEOPLE

It is not only people as individuals that Christ inspires through His resurrection power. He also empowers us as groups, perhaps even more than as individuals. This is never more so than when we join together as Christ's resurrection people, the Church. I once heard my friend, one of the world's foremost missionary statesmen, John Haggai, tell the amazing story of resurrection power at work not just in one person but in a group of people who joined hands together to serve the Lord. The members of the Young Nak Church began meeting together for worship and Bible study in 1946. They were twenty-seven destitute North Korean refugees and they met in a threadbare tent on a mountain outside Seoul. One Sunday the weight of a heavy snow caused their tent to finally collapse. In that setting their young pastor suggested they build a building to establish a church that would reach out to all the people around them.

For a penniless congregation, that seemed impossible. Some might even have called it an absurd idea. Then one woman in that little congregation demonstrated her commitment. She said,

"I have no money but here is my wedding ring. Sell it and put whatever money you receive towards our new church building."

Another said, "I own only these clothes I wear and the quilt I sleep under. Please take my quilt and sell it, too. I will ask my friend if I may sleep under her quilt while she is awake."

Someone else said, "I have only my spoon and rice bowl. Please take it and sell it. I will borrow my friend's spoon and rice bowl." These sacrificial gifts and others like them were sold and the seemingly meager sale proceeds were invested in advancing Christ's kingdom.

As often happens when God is at work, money came in from unexpected sources. It was added to funds received from the sale of those personal items. In time a new church building was constructed. Much of the work was performed by members of the congregation. Their building was no fancy cathedral, but compared to an old canvas tent it looked splendid to the members of the budding congregation. Even more wonderful was the spirit they sensed God was developing in their midst. It was the Spirit of their resurrected Lord, and they would need it because all that lay ahead did not bode well for that young and growing group of believers.

In 1950, just as the new building was about to be dedicated, Communists from North Korea moved south. They confiscated the church building and transformed it into their ammunition depot. They declared that anyone who came near would be shot. People from that congregation wept as they prayed—from a distance—for God's guidance.

After United Nations forces pushed the Communists back behind the 38th Parallel, a godly elder was permitted by United Nations soldiers to enter the now much abused building and assess its condition. No one knew that some Communist soldiers were still hiding inside. When that elder entered the building the Communists set upon him from behind. They put a gun to his head. He asked for permission to pray. It was granted. He kneeled. They shot him. Realizing their presence was revealed by the gunshot, the Communist soldiers ran away. Now his tombstone marks the spot where that church family found their beloved elder's body. It was the very place where he kneeled to pray.

Financial hardship, sacrifice, opposition, martyrdom, all these have been faced by the Young Nak congregation. Christ's resurrection power has sustained and inspired them in the face of all these things. Today, Young Nak Church is the largest Presbyterian congregation in the world!

HIS RESURRECTION POWER AND OURS!

"Before long, the world will not see me anymore, but you will see me. Because I live, you also will live."[50] Resurrection power! It is often simply the power to hang in when the going gets tough. In the tradition of Young Nak Church and in the tradition of the first disciples, today's disciples ask God's help to demonstrate it to our world.

We believe in the resurrected Jesus and we invite all whose past is marked by evidence of deadness to surrender that past to Him, to watch Him transform it into something new, beautiful and powerful, and to come and join us in our fellowship of service in His name.

OUR HIGHEST PRIORITY:
TO DEMONSTRATE CHRIST'S LOVE

Romans 5:8
"God demonstrates his own love for us in this:
While we were still sinners, Christ died for us."

This is a true story. When Warden Lewis Lawes came to Sing Sing in 1920, he inherited the most despicable place on this continent. Warden Lawes immediately introduced reforms that treated the prisoners like people instead of things. The inmates noticed the difference right away. When they expressed gratitude, Lawes directed the credit to his wife, Kathryn. Kathryn Lawes was a disciple of Jesus and believed Christ's redemption could transform any life.

Sometimes Kathryn took her three children to visit inmates who had no visitors. They were rapists, murderers, and some of the most notorious gangsters in American history. In spite of that, she never showed fear. She encouraged prisoners known to be undergoing a particular difficulty by extending a personal touch in some thoughtful way.

In 1937, seventeen years after the Laweses arrived at Sing Sing, a car accident took Kathryn Lawes' life. The next day her casket lay in the Warden's house a quarter mile from the prison compound. At exercise time the Deputy Warden noticed the prisoners were not gathering in groups or playing basketball, as they usually did. Instead, they gathered silently around the fence that faced the home. Some of the men looked as though they were praying. He knew what they were thinking.

Leaving his station, the Deputy Warden stepped before the prisoners and said, "Men, I'm going to trust you. You may go to the house." He ordered the main gate opened. The prisoners walked through the gate respectfully. No count was taken. No roll was called. No guards were dispatched. That evening at countdown not one prisoner was missing. Love for one who demonstrated love for them made murderers, rapists, con-artists, and gangsters people to be trusted.

Such is the amazing hope we find in the gospel. *"God demonstrates his own love for us in this: While we were still sinners, Christ died for us."* Paul's declaration brings us face to face with Calvary's cross as the masterwork of God's redeeming love.

Having considered the proclamational priority of the Mission Statement in chapters four and five, we come now to its practical priority.

We stand steadfastly for:
Our Foundation . . . the Bible, God's Word;
Our Lord . . . Jesus Christ, God's only Son;
Our highest priority . . . to proclaim
Christ's cross and resurrection;
and demonstrate God's love

As Deep As Faith Gets

Scholarly research confirms that the apostle John, who gave us the Gospel that bears his name, lived to a ripe old age. He was in all likelihood the last of the apostles to die. In the course of his long life, he made many missionary journeys to newly established churches. Imagine how excited the people of those fledgling congregations must have been to welcome him. This was more than an ordinary visiting preacher or theologian. This was *"The disciple whom Jesus loved,"*[31] the final first-hand witness to the resurrection and quite likely Christ's best friend. John was chosen to accompany the Lord to the meeting with Moses and Elijah on the Mount of Transfiguration and later when the Lord went into Gethsemane to pray on the evening before His trial and crucifixion. He saw all this with his own eyes.

One tradition tells of Christians eagerly gathering around the wise old John to listen to his teaching. His lesson was always the same. It was brief and to the point. "Little children, love one another." Having said those few words John would sit down. Sometimes the new Christians were confused. Some were a little miffed. They had, after all, looked forward enthusiastically to John's visit. Was this all they would hear from the great theologian and writer who was selected to write the gospel of God's love for the world?

Finally, one day a relatively young and erudite disciple felt emboldened to speak. "Dear brother," he began, "we already know this, having read and heard it many times before. Might you not be able to give us something just a little deeper?"

"My dear children," John replied, "our Lord's command is that we love one another. It simply does not get any deeper."

There is no confirmed record of this conversation. It is simply one of the traditions of the church. Is it a myth or the truth? We have no way of knowing. But we do know that John's focus on the heart of Christ's teaching is as valid now as it ever was. Our Lord's command to love is at the same time the easiest and the hardest lesson we will ever learn as Christians.

Therefore, proclamation by itself is not enough. No, not even when it is the proclamation of the greatest news the world will ever hear: the wonder of Christ's cross and resurrection. The world we live in demands more than mere words and so it should. Therefore, we also must prioritize the practice of God's love as an ongoing part of the ministry we share.

Where Is God's Love?

There are some things that cause reasonable people to question God's love. Where, for example, is a loving God when little children starve in Biafra?

Where was God when Flight 427 barreled into the hillside near Pittsburgh International Airport? Or, when TWA Flight 800 broke apart and fell into Long Island Sound?

How was God's love demonstrated when an Amish baby died at Children's Hospital a couple of months ago?

Or, when a fifteen-year old was blinded by a gunshot fired by another fifteen-year old in a Pittsburgh neighborhood?

Or, when a campus minister with a wife and young children was murdered while he was coming home from a Bible study at Carnegie Mellon University?

Where was God when a six-year-old beauty queen was molested and strangled in her own home at Christmas?

Where was God when students at Columbine High School in Colorado were being shot for professing faith in Him? Or when an angry mad man mowed down worshippers at Wedgewood Baptist Church in Texas?

Or, when a young man went on a Friday afternoon shooting rampage that left five people dead and another one paralyzed in the suburbs of Pittsburgh?

Where was God on that infamous day of all America's date with the devil, September 11, 2001, when thousands of people on land and in the air were senselessly and cruelly murdered at the Pentagon and World Trade Center Towers and in Somerset County, Pennsylvania?

Rational people, people of good will, ask such questions and who can blame them?

Daily reports in hometown newspapers and on television in every major American city seem to contradict this truth we all want to trust. Yet the death of God's Son on Calvary's cross overshadows every one of them. *"God demonstrates his own love for us in this: While we were still sinners, Christ died for us."* In this Scripture declaration we find the nearest thing to an answer available to us now.

These words do not imply that because of Christ's death our tears are dried away instantly; or that problems disappear into thin air because we believe what Paul writes here. God's love for us does not make us immune to suffering.

Non-Christians and Christians alike question these events because they impact the lives of us all. In many of the instances just cited Christians were the victims of suffering and loss. There is no difference between us at this point. What hurts unbelievers hurts believers also. The darkness of loss still blinds us. Nevertheless, we are satisfied to know that our questions will find their answers in the morning of eternal brightness that in Christ God procured for us on the cross. Circumstances and situations arise for which none of us has perfect answers. And anyone who tells you he does is not playing straight with you.

What we do have is confidence. Jesus said He would never forsake us and we take Him at His word. That does not mean we escape loss or suffering. It means that God Himself will never leave us no matter what we face. As Christians, we believe the answer is on its way. The day will come when we will understand all these things. Meanwhile, *"We see but a poor reflection as in a mirror; then we shall see face to face."*[32] All we have to rely on until then is the Bible's constant assurance that God really does love us. The supreme proof of that love is the death of God's Son for us.

EVERYDAY LOVE

Do not miss this love's everyday nature. Paul does not speak of a past-tense love. He does not write that love was demonstrated. He writes that love is being demonstrated now. There is a perpetual present tense to it. God "demonstrates," says the apostle.

Some Bible statements are historical. They happened once, achieved their purpose, and were put away, as it were. *"The LORD shut (Noah) in (the ark).*"[33] That happened only once, a long time ago. A lot has happened in the meantime. Yet one fact about God stands unmoved every day. At the core of all things, unshaken and unshakable, is God's Calvary love.

This love that God demonstrates for us is more than a Good Friday afternoon romance. It is the most living love story ever. In each and every generation it transforms people who do bad things into children of God. It gives those with no respect, self-respect, and those with no life, life eternal. It says that no matter what others think about us, Christ favors us before Himself. To those the world deems worthless it says that He values you more than all the wealth in the universe. God loves you today. And that is a fact.

It is this present-tense nature that calls us to demonstrate Christ's love. It is not enough merely to tell people that God loves them in Jesus or that one day they will see just how much God loves them.

We are called to show them God's love in Christ, here and now, every day. That is why we make this our priority in ministry.

THE NATURE OF GOD'S LOVE

There are many kinds of love. One builds up, exalts, and seeks the best for its beloved while another drags its beloved down to its own level. One love is nothing but lust disguised, while another dreams the best for its beloved and does all it can to help make that dream happen.

The love of God is infinitely greater than the best of human love. His love is a love with no limits that deems no price too great to pay. It is a love all sufficient it leaves nothing for us to do but believe it with all our heart. Isn't that amazing? There are no conditions to the way God loves us. All we must do to experience His love is trust Him for it.

Turn your focus to Calvary's cross. See the scene there. Who was that with pierced hands and feet hanging between two thieves, but God's only Son? No patriot ever loved like that. Nor did any mother, though a healthy mother-love must surely be the nearest thing we can know to it. No human love can ever compare to Christ Jesus willingly hanging in shame before a mocking mob for the sake of others. His love that day was, and still is, wide enough to embrace every person ever born and long enough to go with us however far we wander. It was deep enough to stretch down into hell and high enough to raise us to all God wills for us.

A New England couple announced their engagement only a few weeks before America entered the Second World War. Wedding plans were postponed by the country's call. At the station as he boarded the train that would take him toward basic training, they pledged to write daily letters to each other, which they did. As each letter arrived she read it and dreamed of the day he would come back from the war.

Then, without warning, his letters stopped coming. "I'll get one tomorrow," she thought at first. Still, weeks went by and no letters came. She took the letters he had written from the drawer, where she kept each treasured one, and untied the ribbon that held them together. She read and re-read every sentence. It was not the same as getting a new letter every day, but it was something to hold to in hope that another letter might come soon.

Finally, a letter came. His name and number were on the envelope but the writing was different. She ripped the envelope apart and found one sheet inside. One sheet! One sheet that ripped away her dreams.

He wrote, "Something has happened and I have terrible news for you. I was severely wounded in battle and have lost both my arms. Someone else writes this for me. I love you as much as ever, but feel I must release you from the obligation of our engagement. Move on with your life. You will be better off without me."

Tears rolled off her cheeks and blotched the ink as she read his letter again. She took pen and paper in hand, but could find no words to answer. It was too hard. She decided not to write back. Instead, at the station where once they kissed goodbye, she boarded a train for New York. Once there, she purchased a ticket on a ship headed for Europe. In a strange land she found her way to the military hospital named on that envelope. Tearfully, she searched among the wounded and dying for the man who had given her his ring. When she found him, she threw her arms around his neck, kissed him, and said, "From this day forward, my arms are your arms, just as my heart is yours. I will take care of you always. There is nothing that we cannot do together."

Love In Theory Versus Love In Reality

In Berkeley, California, I was told about a scholarly confirmed bachelor who wrote a treatise on the theme "What Is Love?" His research was extensive, lasting several months. It involved hours of interviews, listening to lectures, and reading books in the library. After gathering his material he prepared his work for presentation. He called a stenography service and asked that someone come to his study to type his manuscript. Soon after that a young woman arrived to do that work. As they encountered each other for the first time something unexpected and unusual happened. Their eyes met. Both of them felt a strange feeling sweep through them. Their pulses quickened. It was love at first sight. Suddenly the subject of that bachelor's paper was more than just an academic project to him. In one exciting meeting he learned more about love than all the research in the world could ever teach him.

So it is with God's love. It must be more than theory to us. We must relax ourselves in His presence and let Him communicate His love to us. When we do His love becomes our own and we know that although *"God so loved the world that he gave his one and only Son, that whoever believes in him shall not perish but have eternal life."*[34] He would love us all alone if we were the only person in the world. Having experienced that love personally it becomes our duty, no more than that, it becomes our delight to pass it on to others in Christ's name.

Thus we demonstrate His love for we know that God has no arms but our arms with which to embrace those who feel unloved. He has no heart but our hearts to love the lost, the lonely, the broken, and the wounded people in our generation. If there is one thing more wonderful than to know personally this love of God we receive every day in Jesus, it must surely be that He invites us to pass it on for Him.

The Mission Statement says, *"Our highest priority is to proclaim Christ's cross and resurrection and demonstrate His love"* because these faith principles of proclamation and practice are inseparably linked. Words without action are a sign of arrogance. In the apostle Paul's words, they make us no more than *"clanging cymbals."*[35]

The Mission Statement announces an intention to make this declaration more than a noble high-sounding sentence by putting shoe leather on it. This is a worthy goal for all who follow Jesus. As we link arms and hearts with other Christians there is nothing we cannot do together for Him who loved us all the way to Calvary's cross and loves us still.

Our Ultimate Goal: That All May Know The Saving Power of the Gospel

John 3:16-18,36

"For God so loved the world that he gave his one and only Son, that whoever believes in him shall not perish but have eternal life. For God did not send his Son into the world to condemn the world, but to save the world through him. Whoever believes in him is not condemned, but whoever does not believe stands condemned already because he has not believed in the name of God's one and only Son . . . Whoever believes in the Son has eternal life, but whoever rejects the Son will not see life, for God's wrath remains on him."

〜〜〜

A parable pictures billions of people scattered on a great plane before God's judgment throne at the end of the world. This is the ultimate final examination. Some huddle and pray fervently for mercy. Some collude to make excuses for their misdeeds. Others talk belligerently. The heightened volume of their uneasy voices is easily heard above the others, "How can God judge us?" one agitated voice asks. "What does He understand about what we have suffered?"

Suddenly a woman from the latter group rolls up her shirtsleeve and reveals her Auschwitz tattoo. At the same time she lifts her voice angrily, "What can God who sits in heaven know about the beatings, torture, and death our people endured in the prison camps?"

An African-American man's open shirt collar exposes an ugly rope burn. He unbuttons another button to make it easier for others to see. "We suffocated in slave ships and toiled in hot sun until death was our best hope for freedom," he cries out. "We were lynched for being black. What can God know about the evils of racism?"

Another man declares, "I'll tell you, God can never understand how lucky He has it to live a sheltered life with no tears, fear, hunger, nor hatred."

From the membership of this group a coalition is appointed to seek common ground. One is chosen to represent each concern present that day. The final composition of the association they form includes a Jew, an African-American, an Indian Untouchable, an illegitimate person, and a homeless person. Together they plan their defense and prepare to present their case succinctly.

Before God can be our judge, they say, let Him experience something of our suffering on Earth. He must be willing to live on Earth as a man. Let Him be a Jew of the under classes, born under such circumstance that people would question His legitimacy. Charge Him to champion some unpopular, but just cause and experience the hate-filled response of a status quo determined to destroy him. In the face of that, He must work for peace. Toward the end, let Him experience betrayal by a trusted close friend and be indicted on false charges. Drag Him before a prejudiced jury and cowardly judge who will turn Him over to be punished even though He did nothing wrong. Throw Him in prison where He will endure beatings at the hands of cowards who will care not at all that He is unarmed and unable to defend Himself. Take Him, at last, to the public square to endure complete abandonment, public humiliation, and the most ignoble death society can imagine.

Their list completed, the belligerent mob's leaders read it aloud before their followers. As they read it, deadly silence falls over them all. Apart from the readers, no one says a word. No one protests. No one scorns. No one moves. Instead, they hang their heads in shame for they realize that God in Jesus Christ has already served their sentence. They can catalog no punishment nor injustice which He had not already suffered.

"God did not send his Son into the world to condemn the world, but to save the world through him."

OUR ULTIMATE GOAL

We stand steadfastly for:
Our Foundation . . . the Bible, God's Word;
Our Lord . . . Jesus Christ, God's only Son;
Our highest priority . . . to proclaim
Christ's cross and resurrection;
and demonstrate His love;
Our Highest Goal . . . that all may know
the saving power of the Gospel . . .

Everything we have said so far is directed toward an objective or focused on a goal. That goal has two parts to it. Those parts form the subject of this chapter and the one that follows. The first part of our goal is, *"That all may know the saving power of the Gospel."*

THE SAVING POWER OF THE GOSPEL

If we focus on this tenet alone, we will be in increasingly rare company even among the churches. If today's church in our nation and in many parts of the world is deficient in one area more than any other, it is that this most central Scriptural command of passing on our faith by word and deed is largely disregarded. We have lost the sense of urgency that once caused us to focus on evangelism and missions as every Christian's central focus. Many major mainline denominations are losing members as a result. It is sad but true that the vast majority of Christians die without ever having offered themselves to lead another person to saving faith in Christ.

What is the saving power of the gospel? The Bible speaks of it under three powerful concepts: Justification, Sanctification, Glorification.

THE PAST TENSE: WE WERE SAVED

In the past, we were saved. God *"chose us in Christ before the creation of the world"* Paul tells the church at Ephesus in his epistle.[56] He writes in the past tense *"God chose us . . ."* to establish an already accomplished action.

Through this already accomplished action on God's part we have been justified. To be justified is to be declared "just-as-if-I'd" never sinned. The key word in this context is "declared." It is not that we are sinless but that God has proclaimed us so. Neither does it mean that we no longer sin but, rather, that we *"Rejoice in God through our Lord Jesus Christ, through whom we have now received reconciliation."*[57] Notice again that Paul uses the past tense to pass this gospel truth to us. This enables us to know that our reconciliation to God is an already accomplished fact.

There was a day when despite our sin God treated everyone of us who trusts in Christ as though we were sinless. He certified us to be innocent. Some Christians remember the very moment they heard this good news for the first time. They can tell the exact time, date, and place they realized they were forgiven. Others may not have that recollection because they were raised in the faith and put their trust in Christ for forgiveness before their memory processes fully comprehended what happened. Whatever the case, all of us surely remember when we realized that God graciously included us in Christ's atoning death.

Jackie grew up in the church. As a child of the covenant she received baptism in infancy. She learned later that the baptism took place during her first trip out after she was released from the newborn unit at the hospital. Before the congregation of God's people, her parents presented her and pledged to raise her in the nurture and admonition of the Lord, to teach her the great verities of the Christian faith, and to pray with and for her. They kept their promise with great faithfulness. From her earliest days Jackie was aware of Christ's love for her. She does not remember exactly when she asked Jesus to come into her heart. What she does remember, however, is that when she was in college she gradually came to an understanding of precisely what that meant in terms of her eternal soul and God's claim on her life. She says, "After months of trying to figure it out, it finally all came together for me. My heart leaped inside me and I knew that God had called me His own and nothing could ever separate me from His love." She knew in that instant that she must spend her life in service to Christ. Today she nurses sick children at a mission hospital in East Africa.

The line from a great old gospel hymn fits her story perfectly:

> *He loved me e'er I knew Him,*
> *And all my love is due Him*

Jackie found the victory that Christ alone provided when He saved her on Calvary's cross. She came with the faith of a child, and God nurtured that faith within her heart until the moment she realized that Christ had been in her life before she even knew it.

Others tell a different story. Francis of Assisi was born into a wealthy Italian family in 1182. Because of his inherited wealth and loose spirit Francis saw little need for an education. Preferring parties to school, he received only a few years of formal education and spent his early

76

life as a playboy. Duty to country called and Francis enlisted in the army. His position in society guaranteed him an immediate commission to officer status but it did not guarantee his safety in battle. Captured by the enemy, he spent a year as a prisoner-of-war. While in prison he fell ill and feared he might die. In that context he surrendered his life to Christ.

It was an amazing conversion experience. Francis, who had little use for education before, now read every book he could find. Learning about the encounter between Jesus and the rich young ruler through reading the Bible, Francis promised God that if his life was spared, he would give everything he had to help the poor.

Long before San Francisco, a city named in his honor, opened its Golden Gate, Saint Francis opened the gate to his gold. True to his word, upon his release from prison Francis sold all his possessions, including his shoes. He spent the money he made from the sale of his earthly possessions caring for others. He was left with only the set of clothes he was wearing. His parents were convinced their son was mentally ill. Francis' father, Pietro, concerned that his son would give away the entire family fortune, disinherited him. Even that could not cool Francis' commitment to serving Christ. He supported himself by repairing chapels around Assisi. People who knew the playboy Francis before his conversion observed the difference Christ brought about in his life. Many of his former playboy friends were so impressed by his new-found concern for the sick and needy that they followed Francis' example and sacrificed their own wealth for the gospel. Thus began the Order of the Begging Brothers.

This band of former party-boys went out two by two spreading Christ's message of new life and service. They took their message throughout Italy, France, Germany, Hungary, Spain, and England. Wherever they went they preached the gospel and established hospitals and schools in Christ's name.

Later Francis formed an order—known as the Order of the Poor Clares—for his former female playmates who also sought to make a difference in Christ's name. The original "Clare" was a wealthy young socialite whose parents gave her that name at birth. Like Francis, she also sold everything she possessed to follow Jesus.

Two years after Francis died in 1226, Pope Gregory IX canonized him as an official saint of the church. Soon after, the Order of the Begging Brothers became the Order of St. Francis or the Franciscans. Twenty years after Francis' death his order had constructed more than 9,000 homes, hospitals, and schools.

For Jackie the knowledge of being saved came gradually. For Francis of Assisi it came suddenly. Yet the results were the same; a life was transformed and dedicated to serving the King of Kings. Such is the difference Christ makes through the saving power of the gospel. *"For it is by grace you have been saved, through faith—and this not from yourselves, it is the gift of God—not by works, so that no one can boast. For we are God's workmanship, created in Christ Jesus to do good works, which God prepared in advance for us to do."*[38]

No one can seriously consider what it means to be saved by God through Christ's sacrifice and remain disinterested, unconcerned, and uninvolved in making Christ's message known.

THE PRESENT TENSE: WE ARE BEING SAVED

Writing to the church at Corinth, Paul addresses his message *"To us who are being saved."*[39] Here the imperfect tense of the Greek verb signifies an action that, although incomplete, is under way. In a sense God's "Work in Progress" sign hangs on each of our lives. Sanctification is under way as another work of God's free grace. Once we were saved from sin's penalty. Now we are being saved from sin's power. We are not yet perfect for, in Francis Shaeffer's words, "If you'll only settle for perfection or nothing, you'll always end up with nothing." *"Sin shall not be your master, because you are not under law, but under grace."*[60]

Perhaps no part of Scripture makes this more plain than Paul's confession to the Romans, *"What I do is not the good I want to do; no, the evil I do not want to do—this I keep on doing."*[61] These words frame the story of Paul's personal struggle after his conversion to Christ. If you are real, they tell your story, too. All who belong to Christ live between two worlds. One is the world that now is. The other is the world we aspire to make for Him who loved us all the way to Calvary and who loves us still.

THE FUTURE TENSE: WE SHALL BE SAVED

"Since we have now been justified by his blood, how much more shall we be saved from God's wrath through him!"[62] We were saved from sin's penalty. That is salvation's past tense. We are being saved from sin's power. This is salvation's present tense. One day, we shall be saved even from sin's presence. Christ has prepared a sinless environment for us in eternity. This is God's promise concerning our salvation's future tense. The salvation that was begun in eternity past and was consummated on Calvary's cross

continues to work in us through our sanctification. It will be completed hereafter in our glorification.

Justification! Sanctification! Glorification! The three tenses of salvation. In Paul's words, *"Those He predestined, He also called; those He called, He also justified; those He justified, He also glorified."*63 *"From the beginning God chose you to be saved through the sanctifying work of the Spirit and through belief in the truth" (2 Thessalonians 2:13)*. In theology, the queen of the sciences, these are three key components of what we call the "Ordo Salutis," the order of salvation.

WHAT ARE WE SAVED FROM?

Sadly, too often neither our culture nor the church squares with this issue. *"Whoever rejects the Son will not see life, for God's wrath remains on him."* We are saved from God's anger. We who are saved will not endure His final punishment. This is what gives us the imperative in our preaching, teaching, and ministry.

An elderly Russian woman devoutly kissed the feet of a statue of Christ in the presence of a Soviet soldier. The soldier immediately challenged her with this question, "Babushka, will you kiss Stalin's feet?"

"Of course," she replied, "as soon as he dies for me, rises again, and says he still loves me!" That dear woman understood the gospel and what Christ did for us.

ARE YOU SAVED?

"Brother, are you saved? Sister, are you saved?" Comedians, even some who say they are Christians, make fun of those questions. The world makes caricatures of them. In spite of that we must always remember, *"Salvation is found in no one else, for there is no other name under heaven given to men by which we must be saved."*[64]

Are You Saving?

Only Christ can save and He enlists us in His service with the privilege of telling His salvation plan. Most often, it seems God uses more than one person to introduce someone to new life in Jesus Christ. Yet, the fact remains that we are all charged with telling the lost how to be saved. We may be the first or the second person to tell someone. We may be the twentieth, or thirtieth, or fiftieth; or, we may be the last—the one who actually sees someone receive Christ by faith. What number we are is not important. What is eternally important is that we accept our assignment to be a witness for the saving power of the Gospel of Christ Jesus.

How long has it been since you last invited someone to receive the Lord or to join you where you knew Christ's claim on every life would be presented? We have been made stewards of God's good news and good news is worth sharing. Therefore, *"Each one should use whatever gift he has received to serve others, faithfully administering God's grace in its various forms. If anyone speaks, he should do it as one speaking the very words of God. If anyone serves, he should do it with the strength God provides, so that in all things God may be praised through Jesus Christ. To him be the glory and the power for ever and ever. Amen."*[65]

A Life Worthy of
Christ's Calling

2 Thessalonians 1:11
*"We constantly pray for you, that our God may
count you worthy of his calling, and that by his
power he may fulfill every good purpose of yours
and every act prompted by your faith."*

⚓

From time to time the media bring news of some cult that
misunderstands the central thrust of Christ's message and
our responsibility. Usually such movements are confused by
a hodgepodge theology that, because it was not corrected in a
timely and constructive fashion, lost its balance. One such movement was the Heavens Gate group whose people settled near
San Diego, California, and awaited the arrival of the Hale-Bopp
comet, which they believed would deliver them from this world
altogether. Another was the Jim Jones group that settled for a
time in seclusion in Guyana and waited there believing the Lord
would come soon for them. There are many others. Who among

us has not thought at some time of "running away from it all?" The peaceful seclusion that life alone, or perhaps with a few specially chosen friends or family members, seems to offer can seem very appealing to the human imagination. The words of the old Country Western song, "This world is not my home, I'm just a-passin' through," have a place in all our hearts from time to time. Life, perhaps particularly for serious disciples of Jesus, is not easy in this world and escape seems not unattractive when times are tough. Yet, Christ never calls us to separate ourselves from the world. Indeed, the Lord who was *"tempted in every way, just as we are"*[66] specifically cautions us against the potential perils of isolationism. *"No branch can bear fruit by itself; it must remain in the vine. Neither can you bear fruit unless you remain in me."*[67] Because the Thessalonian Christians also were familiar with the temptation to look for a way out of this world, Paul wrote them a letter that was intensely practical for them and is just as practical for us today.

In a sense Paul's second Thessalonian letter can be called a corrective for its predecessor; not because First Thessalonians is incorrect, but because parts of it were misunderstood and misinterpreted by those Christians to whom it was initially addressed. In the first letter Paul wrote powerfully comforting and encouraging words about Christ's Second Coming. Paul's words so captured the imagination of many Thessalonians that they believed the day of Christ's return was so imminent and many of them stopped working their regular jobs to await His appearing. Now Paul, having heard this, wrote from Corinth some months after the first letter to clarify this misunderstanding and to encourage the Thessalonian Christians, and us, to focus on practical Christian living. As he does in other places, Paul sets us a model for how to deal with difficult issues in the church. He responds quickly with words that are firm and encouraging.

Good News Travels Fast

Paul recognized the far-reaching implications of anything that happened in Thessalonica in his day. This seaport city lying at the foothills of Mount Khortiatis, had an impact far beyond other cities of similar size when Paul established a church there. Then, as now, it was known as a gem of the ocean. A prosperous port and trading center, it was a recognized place for people to gather and discuss the things that were on their minds and hearts. In a crude kind of way, Thessalonica was CNN Central. Thessalonica was, therefore, an information center. Ships from all over the world docked there to load and unload cargo. The sailors who traveled on those ships took news from Thessalonica all over the world, whether it was good or bad. Needless to say, misinformation and misunderstanding about the gospel in a place like that could have far reaching consequences. On the other hand, good news well-told would also travel far making a positive mark on many lives. So, when Paul writes his second letter he does so with a sense of urgency. He sees the potential for rapidly spreading Christ's good news.

He tells the Thessalonians that Jesus may indeed return at any moment. Therefore, Christians must live in a state of readiness, prepared to greet the Lord at any moment. On the other hand, Jesus may tarry. It could be a long time by human reckoning before He returns. If He delays, the people of the church need to consider how to live in the meantime. *"With this in mind, we constantly pray for you, that our God may count you worthy of his calling, and that by his power he may fulfill every good purpose of yours and every act prompted by your faith."*[68]

A Life Worthy of Christ's Calling

We stand steadfastly for:
Our Foundation . . . the Bible, God's Word;
Our Lord . . . Jesus Christ, God's only Son;
Our highest priority . . . to proclaim
Christ's cross and resurrection;
Our Highest Goal . . . that all may know
the saving power of the Gospel
and live a life worthy of Christ's calling

In the World But Not Of It

In some ways the Mission Statement phrase we are considering in this chapter might be called the tough part of our life together in Christ. It calls us to something that, at least for now, seems humanly impossible. *"Live a life worthy of Christ's calling."* The key word is live. As Christians we are called to live in the present world. However, we are called to not live like this world. A life worthy of our Lord's calling means we do not disconnect ourselves from life in this present world. We do, however, come apart from those things which the world does that dishonor Christ and break God's commandments. We become salt and light bringing a positive influence wherever we can in our society.

So, also, this phrase might be called our Mission Statement's practical phrase. In that sense it is the easiest one to keep, for how we are to keep it is spelled out in the Mission Statement itself. In a generation that often seems to be lost in a spiritual and moral fog, it clearly declares who we are. These words tell all who see them or hear them that this is who we plan to be until Christ returns. God helping us, this is where we will stand for Christ and for Christ alone. We will be people whose only foundation is the Bible, which we receive as God's Word. Our Lord shall be Jesus Christ, God's only Son, and no other. Our first priority is to proclaim Christ's cross and resurrection. Our supreme goal is that people everywhere may know the saving power of the Gospel of Jesus Christ who alone is worthy to save and that they may live a life worthy of His calling.

GRACE AT WORK

Paul opens his letter by commending the Christians of Thessalonica for their growing faith: *"Your faith is growing more and more."*[69] As the founding pastor of the church in Thessalonica, nothing brings Paul more joy than news of faith growing there.

Every pastor feels a sense of great delight and fulfillment when this happens. Not long ago, I taught a Bible study to a young adult group. Their attentive listening, astute questions, and absorbing spirits brought me great delight. Memories of that evening have caused my soul to soar each time I have thought about it. May God be praised for what He is doing among us!

PRACTICAL LOVE

Paul's commendation to the Thessalonian Christians continues with another word of gratitude. *"The love everyone of you has for each other is increasing."*[70] Wherever the true church of Christ meets love is always in the air. *"By this all men will know that you are my disciples, if you love one another."*[71] Eleven times the New Testament calls for this demonstration of love between the people of God as a required part of what it means to be one of the Lord's disciples.

Now, the love Christ decrees among us is not some sloppy emotion than runs high and low according to our mood of the moment. It is perhaps best demonstrated by a constant spirit of caring for others within Christ's body, the church, and by genuine concern among us when we learn about someone's need of friendship, fellowship, support, or other life necessity. Paul saw this same spirit at work in Thessalonica and commended the Christians there for this evidence of a life worthy of Christ's calling.

Perseverance Under Pressure

Another evidence of Christ's work for which Paul commends these Christians is their spirit of stick-to-it-iveness. *"We boast about your perseverance and faith in all the persecutions and trials you are enduring."*[72] For *perseverance* Paul chooses *hupome*, a strong Greek word meaning more than mere idle endurance. This word *hupome* means these Christians understand suffering in the context of blessings and respond to it in constructive ways.

True suffering is a gift from God. *"It has been granted to you on behalf of Christ not only to believe on him, but also to suffer for him."*[73] Suffering understood in this light provides an opportunity for us to steadfastly demonstrate our Christian mettle. Something in our nature does not readily consider suffering a privilege. Yet, nothing demonstrates Christ's presence in us quite like the way we face suffering. Adversity tells more about our commitment to the Lord of the cross than all the Bibles we can carry under our arms. It is said that the blood of the martyrs is the seed of the church. Christian history certainly demonstrates this. Every century records testimonies about Christians thriving in suffering. How we face tough times is the evidence of a *"life worthy of his calling"* being lived out in us.

THE RIGHTEOUS JUDGMENT OF GOD

Contrary to what some people think, preachers do not enjoy talking about fire and brimstone. Jeremiah wept at the thought of it. Jesus did too as He peered over Jerusalem. Emotionally healthy people have no joy thinking about the judgment of others. Having said that, however, any preacher who fails to deal with the subject when Scripture raises it is being unfaithful to Christ's call. Paul tells the Thessalonians that there is a present judgment and a future judgment. *"All this is evidence that God's judgment is right."*[74] He chooses words in the present tense indicating that this judgment is here and now.

We have already seen that our responses to God ("growing faith"), to one another ("increasing love"), and to adversity ("positive perseverance") tell the world that Christ is doing His work in us to make us worthy of His calling. This, says the apostle, also indicates that God is making good decisions concerning us.

In addition to this present judgment, Paul writes that God also has a future judgment in mind. His words move to the future tense. *"God is just: He will pay back trouble to those who trouble you."*[75] We see cruelty and unfairness all across the world. Where is fairness? Where is equity? Good people ask these questions. The Bible message is clear: God's arm is not short. His judgment may not always be swift by our standards, but it is always sure. Those who make trouble for His children will reap a bitter harvest and that without exception.

Intercessory Prayer

Paul says that Christ's revelation of Himself among the Thessalonians will bring judgment on the unsaved, rest for the saved, and glory for the Lord through His people. He then offers a prayer of intercession for these Christians. It is this prayer that forms the backdrop for this phrase in the Mission Statement. Paul prays that they may carry on to fruition every resolution for good among them and every work that demonstrates faith. In short, their walk is to be a demonstration of their talk. His hope for them, and surely for us also, is that Christ who will be glorified in His return will also be glorified now in the lives of all who love Him.

This word is a call to practical Christian living in each church and in every generation of Christians. Therefore, we plan our lives now in subservience to the Lord. "A life worthy" means living between now and the time Christ comes, in obedience to Him. My friend, R.C. Sproul, writes a magazine column called *Right Now Counts Forever!* He is right. It does. What we do in the present matters. God reckons it eternally important. Our behavior has lasting consequences.

"That our God may count you worthy . . ." A life worthy of God is not

earned. Like the saving grace of the gospel, it is a free gift. Nobody is capable of getting God's approval through human goodness and efforts. The way we receive God's approval is through appreciating His love and responding to it in practical everyday ways. That is why Paul does not tell these Christians to live a life worthy. He says he prays they will live such a life. We can live such a life only by God's power.

"We make it our goal to please him."[76] In the best selling Christian novel of all time, *In His Steps,* Charles M. Sheldon speaks of the practical living out of the gospel for every Christian disciple. He suggests that we approach each decision and every situation in the context of a simple, yet profoundly spiritual question: "What would Jesus do?" To do what Jesus wants and tells us to do is the daily mission of every disciple.

His Life In Us

What would Jesus do if He were in your place or mine? This question always has validity because Jesus is in our place. *"I have been crucified with Christ and I no longer live, but Christ lives in me. The life I live in the body, I live by faith in the Son of God, who loved me and gave himself for me."*[77] If it is true that "Christ lives in me," then asking how He would act or respond in each circumstance I face is a very practical outworking of His life in me. Through consistent Bible study and prayer God directs us to this question's answer for all of life. In finding the answer and putting it into action we will become the mind, heart, arms, legs, feet, and hands of Jesus in our city and in our world.

Why should we want to do this? Because we love Him and there is a reason for that love. *"We love because he first loved us."*[78] If you have little children in your life you understand this. We love them not because they always behave perfectly but because of who they are. Most of us hope that when our children no longer fear losing our love, they will want to behave in ways that are good, just, and honorable. The same is true in a spiritual sense. When we realize God's love is an act of free grace, not earned, motivated by our obedience, we want to do everything we can to please Him.

God so loved us that He gave up His Son for us. The story of "Baby M" a few years ago illustrates this point from a different perspective. A surrogate mother offered to bear a child for a childless couple. All went well until she saw the child soon after it was born. Suddenly and not surprisingly, a bond developed that no one seemed to have planned for in this case. The childless couple argued that since they initiated the plans and paid all the fees, the baby belonged to them. The mother, however, spoke simply of her love for her child. There is no greater force nor higher motivation for people than love, and popular opinion turned in her favor.

What could I ever do that would motivate you to willingly give up your child for me? Nothing! What would compel you to choose to sacrifice your own child for anyone? Nothing but totally indescribable love. Such is God's love for us. *"God so loved the world that he gave his one and only Son, that whoever believes in him shall not perish but have eternal life."*[79]

What will we do in response to that greatest of all gifts? We will try every way we can to live a life worthy of His calling.

It Takes Time

A great story tells of an aged man, an accomplished artist, who was applying the finishing touches to a bronze sculpture. Day after day he kept on filing, scraping, and polishing every surface of his masterpiece. "When will it be done?" an observer asked him.

"Never," the grand old artist replied. "I just keep on improving it until they come to take it away."

The same can be said of us. Because our salvation is complete in Christ, heaven is our guarantee. Yet, when it comes to being perfect we all have a long way to go. The good news is that God keeps working on us day after day. One day He will come and take us away. After that we will be with Him forever. Until then, we try to remember to demonstrate our trust in Him. An acorn is not made into an oak tree in a day. It takes time. A great scholar is not made wise by one day of schooling. It takes time. One touch of an artist's brush never made a painting a masterpiece. It takes time. Planting seeds happens in a day. Reaping a harvest takes time. Becoming what we are designed to be in Christ does not happen instantly. It takes time. Be encouraged, child of God. Your time will come. The great Sculptor, that Carpenter of Nazareth called Jesus, is putting His finishing touch on you, and one day He will come Himself and take you home to His Father's house.

When Excellence is Not an Option

"With this in mind, we constantly pray for you, that our God may count you worthy of his calling, and that by his power he may fulfill every good purpose of yours and every act prompted by your faith." What a beautiful portrait of the Christian life these words lay before us. Once

we are completely committed to being all Christ dreams for us excellence is not an option. We will never again be satisfied with giving less than our utmost to and for Him. Goodness brings its own pleasure. A great depth of satisfaction comes from doing God's will well that no words can describe and no tongue can tell. Loving acts, gracious words, thoughtful deeds, generous affirmations and enthusiastic service for the Master all work to bring God pleasure. And the result? The mutual glorification of Christ in us in this present time and our final glorification with Him in our Father's house forever and ever.

THEMES TO THINK ON - THINGS TO DO

1. What are some priorities for which your church or organization exists? Write these out clearly.

2. After you have finished your list, lay some plans for how you will accomplish these goals. Write these down and refer to them often—no less than once each week. Establish a means by which you can measure your progress in keeping each one.

PEOPLE WE STAND WITH

PARTNERS TOGETHER IN
PURSUIT OF EXCELLENCE

Our Strength: The Holy Spirit

Zechariah 4:6
*"Not by might nor by power, but by my
Spirit," says the Lord Almighty."*

✎

2 Corinthians 13:14
*"May the grace of the Lord Jesus Christ, and
the love of God, and the fellowship of the Holy
Spirit be with you all."*

✎

Having considered each of the priorities we stand for we now come to the final section of our mission toward excellence. We recognize right away that we are into something that is bigger than any of us, or even than all of us together. We need Someone to stand with us or our mission is doomed to failure. That special Someone is the Holy Spirit, not an "it" but a person.

We stand steadfastly for:
Our Foundation . . . the Bible, God's Word;
Our Lord . . . Jesus Christ, God's only Son;

Our highest priority . . . to proclaim
Christ's cross and resurrection;
Our Highest Goal . . . that all may know
the saving power of the Gospel
and live a life worthy of Christ's calling;
Our Strength . . . The Holy Spirit.

It has already been clearly stated that each priority challenges us to a task too strenuous for any of us to achieve through our own strength. So, we look for a strength beyond ourselves. That strength comes from the Holy Spirit. He is the subject of this chapter.

"Did we in our own strength confide, our striving would be losing," Martin Luther wrote. He is right, of course. It has already been clearly stated that each pillar of the Mission Statement challenges us to a task too strenuous for any of us to achieve in our own strength. So we look for a strength beyond ourselves. That strength comes from the Holy Spirit.

Forty days after He died on the cross and rose again, Jesus ascended into heaven. Nothing was left for us to do to be saved and assured of heaven except to trust Him.

Yet, God's work in the world was not completed, nor is it completed now. Christ established His Church and promised it a supernatural power unlike anything the world had seen before. *"You will receive power when the Holy Spirit comes on you; and you will be my witnesses in Jerusalem, and in all Judea and Samaria, and to the ends of the earth."*[80]

This promise came fully alive ten days after Christ's ascension into heaven and fifty days after He rose from the grave. Jesus sent His Holy Spirit into His Church. This empowerment of His people by the Holy Spirit signaled that Jesus' work was now complete. He came from heaven. Now, having conquered death, He has returned to heaven. Before returning He entrusted us with a message of certain salvation to declare to an uncertain world. The Holy Spirit is God's empowering Agent to bring that message to life in us individually and collectively.

MEDIOCRITY AT BEST

"Attempt something so great for God," John Edmund Haggai once told me, "that it is doomed to failure unless God be in it!" In a sense, that is Haggai's unique paraphrase of the same principle we sing about in Luther's hymn. John Haggai was turning Luther's fear into a positive life principle and pushing it to the far edges of imagination. What would be the most wonderful thing you could imagine doing if there were no limits? If you can dream it, you can do it in the power of the Holy Spirit. Without the Holy Spirit of God we are doomed to mediocrity at best. Yet, no member of the Holy Trinity has suffered more at the hands of those who practice theological quackery than the Holy Spirit. From the old-fashioned snake oil salesman of a century or more ago to today's practitioners of health and wealth theology, the Holy Spirit has been maligned, misrepresented, and misinterpreted. This is unfortunate, yet this is the world in which we live and minister together for Christ's sake.

ISRAEL'S ADVANTAGE:

The God Who Has It All Together

"Hear, O Israel: The LORD our God, the LORD is one."[81] These words called the Shema in Israel form the crux of historic Jewish theology. They declared to the polytheistic nations all around them that Israel was monotheistic. The other nations could choose to have numerous different gods if they wanted, but Israel would have no one but the Lord God.

"Jehovah our LORD is One,"[82] the Shema prophet cried out. An equally acceptable translation would be *"Jehovah our LORD is together."* The Hebrew word *echad*, translated *one*, frequently means a single unit composed of inseparable parts. For example, in Genesis 2:4 it speaks of the man being one with his wife. They are separate personalities yet God regards them as united. Similarly, in Numbers 12:32 *echad* describes the cluster of grapes the spies brought back from Canaan. Although each grape is separate, all finally are joined together at the stem as though they were one. In short, to their neighboring nations, the Israelites through the Shema were saying that Israel needed only one God who would meet every need and they found Him in Jehovah, the Lord of hosts. This particular name for God draws on a military metaphor that declares God as a great army. It says, in effect, that Israel's God is a million man march of one.

The Eternal Love Triangle

"May the grace of the Lord Jesus Christ, and the love of God, and the fellowship of the Holy Spirit be with you all." These are often the concluding words with which we close our worship services. In many ways they are the most important words we can hear be-

cause without the Holy Spirit's fellowship, the Gospel message is powerless for us. Without the Spirit of God we cannot be born again for the Spirit alone enables us to repent and believe the Gospel. Without Him we cannot grow in the knowledge and love of God. Without Him we have no energy to evangelize the lost. Without Him our desire to worship God with our lips and our lifestyle is weak at best.

When Paul the apostle signed off with this benediction in his letter to the Corinthians he probably had no idea that it would be among the most memorable sentences he would ever pen. In addition to being a beautiful benediction, these words also provide us with a wonderfully solid theological statement about the unity of the Godhead. They do so by speaking at the same time about God the Father, God the Son, and God the Holy Spirit. Moreover, they assign the role each One plays in our lives every day.

"The grace of our Lord Jesus Christ" reminds us that Christ's grace is always freely available. We need that for we all sin and find ourselves in need of Christ's forgiveness. *"The love of God"* says that we are always loved by our Father in heaven. Finally, *"The fellowship of the Holy Spirit"* tells us that we have a powerful Friend and Companion traveling with us wherever we go. All of these are a sign of God's tripartite eternal loving nature as Father, Son and Holy Spirit.

David's penetrating question brings both comfort and conviction to us:

Where can I go from your Spirit? Where can I flee from your presence? If

I go up to the heavens, you are there; if I make my bed in the depths, you are there. If I rise on the wings of the dawn, if I settle on the far side of the sea, even there your hand will guide me, your right hand will hold me fast. If I say, 'Surely the darkness will hide me and the light become night around me,' even the darkness will not be dark to you; the night will shine like the day, for darkness is as light to you.[83]

We are loved everywhere for all eternity.

Growing up in Ireland, I learned that back in 1871 Philip P. Bliss wrote a hymn that brings the same sense of comfort to children in every generation:

> *God is always near me,*
> *Hearing what I say,*
> *Knowing all my thoughts and deeds,*
> *All my work and play.*
> *God is always near me;*
> *In the darkest night*
> *He can see me just the same*
> *As by mid-day light.*
> *God is always near me,*
> *Though so young and small;*
> *Not a look or word or thought,*
> *But God knows them all.*

What more could any of us want? We are loved with grace from Jesus. We are loved with a never ceasing love from the Father. Finally, we are loved with ever-near companionship from the Holy Spirit.

WHO IS THE HOLY SPIRIT?

In the course of an otherwise helpful speech, a motivational speaker attempted to describe God's power working in each of our lives to help us achieve success in business. He likened this "power" to the "Force" in the Star Wars movies. Later he closed his talk by quoting a benediction for another threesome—the benediction of the Star Wars trilogy, "May the Force be with you"—without seeming to recognize the difference between the blessing of George Lucas and the eternal God. It is possible to think of the Holy Spirit as nothing more than that, just a force. When we do, however, the force becomes a farce and we miss what Jesus taught us about the Holy Spirit.

The Holy Spirit is a person. That is why we say He is one of the people we stand with. We are careful to say that it is not that He stands with us but that we stand with Him. We do not ask Him to bless what we do so much as we seek to do what He blesses. The Nicean Council, which met in 325 AD, declared, "We believe in the Holy Spirit, the Lord and giver of life, who proceedeth from the Father and the Son." In doing so, the council helped clarify the relationship of the Holy Spirit to God the Father and God the Son.

Jesus taught this too in His farewell talk with the disciples. *"I will ask the Father, and he will give you another Counselor to be with you forever—the Spirit of truth. The world cannot accept him, because it neither sees him nor knows him. But you know him, for he lives with you and will be in you."*84 Christ's choice of the personal pronouns, *him* and *he* and not *it*, makes plain that He regards the Holy Spirit as a person and not merely a power or object.

The Holy Spirit also uses such personal pronouns when He refers to Himself. *"While they were worshiping the Lord and fasting, the Holy Spirit said, 'Set apart for me Barnabas and Saul for the work to which I have called them.' So after they had fasted and prayed, they placed their hands on them and sent them off."*[85] Through these and other Bible passages we safely conclude that God gives us more than a power to accompany and empower us. God gives us a Person who is inseparably connected with the Father and the Son. Thus the Holy Spirit is not only a person but a divine person.

OLDER THAN DIRT

The rural South is a gold mine of quaint verbal expressions. One of my favorites describes a person well along in years: "He is older than dirt."

In truth it can be said of the Holy Spirit that He truly is older than dirt, for the Scripture tells us so. *"In the beginning God created the heavens and the earth. Now the earth was formless and empty, darkness was over the surface of the deep, and the Spirit of God was hovering over the water."*[86] Here we see that the Holy Spirit was present at creation before the earth was formed. The record then adds, *"God said, 'Let the water under the sky be gathered to one place, and let dry ground appear.' And it was so."*[87] First there was the Holy Spirit and then there was the land or dirt.

The point is, of course, that the Holy Spirit has always existed as part of the Trinity. He did not, as some have said or written, begin His existence at Pentecost. He was there at time's beginning and He was present throughout the Old Testament era. The Old Testament quotes Him more than eighty times, each time conveying God's desire to restore and build up.

While God always exists beyond time's confines, it often helps our human understanding if we can grasp some of God's actions within the context of time. In addition to the Spirit's part in creation and the other Old Testament references to His presence, He is also the One who inspired the Old Testament writers.

The Holy Spirit in the New Testament

"The Holy Spirit will come upon you, and the power of the Most High will overshadow you. So the holy one to be born will be called the Son of God."[88] These words announcing the conception of Jesus to Mary, His mother, are the beginning of the Holy Spirit's ministry in the New Testament era. His presence from that announcement to Mary until Pentecost marks a number of milestones in Christ's life. These landmark moments include Jesus' baptism when John the Baptizer saw the Holy Spirit descend like a dove. Later Christ introduced His first sermon in the synagogue by acknowledging the Spirit's presence. *"The Spirit of the Lord is on me, because he has anointed me to preach good news to the poor. He has sent me to proclaim freedom for the prisoners and recovery of sight for the blind, to release the oppressed, to proclaim the year of the Lord's favor."*[89]

On another occasion when Jesus cast out demons, the Pharisees argued that He must do so by the devil, but Jesus quickly corrected that assertion and credited His healing power to the Holy Spirit. Later the writer to the Hebrews said that Christ's entire redemptive ministry was carried on in the power of the Holy Spirit. *"How much more, then, will the blood of Christ, who through the eternal Spirit offered himself unblemished to God, cleanse our consciences from acts that lead to death, so that we may serve the living God!"*[30] What a glorious Savior! What a wonderful Holy Spirit!

THE DAY THE POWER FELL

Then came Pentecost! This marked the beginning of a second era of the Holy Spirit's work, which continues today and will last until the end of the world as we know it. With Pentecost the church was empowered to move beyond the land of Israel into the world. *"You will receive power when the Holy Spirit comes on you; and you will be my witnesses in Jerusalem, and in all Judea and Samaria, and to the ends of the earth."*[31]

There was never before a moment like it in world history, nor has there been one since. People, no matter what their background, heard Peter's sermon instantly translated into their local dialect. It was like those television pictures we have seen when the United Nations is in session and each member wears an earphone that brings the spoken word in his or her own language. Because a translator stands by a microphone translating each speech, the French delegate hears it in French regardless of the language of the speaker; the German delegate hears it spoken in German; and so on. There were, however, no electronic earphones on Pentecost. There was only God's word through God's man empowered by God's Spirit. Peter's message was instantly translated as it traveled through the air from his mouth to each listener's heart without a human translator. The Holy Spirit was the multilingual interpreter of the day. Even more amazing is that each person there not only heard the message in his or her national language but in his or her local dialect.

What an exciting day for church growth that was! Sinners, convicted of their sin, turned to Jesus in masses. Three thousand people were saved one day, five thousand the next, and so forth! The church, now empowered from on high, was on the march and nothing could stop her and nothing will, for Christ said, *"The gates of Hades will not overcome it."*[2]

POWER TO THE PEOPLE

When we lived in the San Francisco Bay Area, we often walked through the Haight Ashbury district where, in the decade of the sixties, the hippies chanted songs that called for power to the people. What they often did not seem to realize was that God already had taken their chant for Himself. He has given His power to us in giving us His Holy Spirit. Jesus says, *"You shall receive power when the Holy Spirit comes upon you."*[3] So great is this power that it is from the Greek root for the English words *dynamic* and *dynamite.*

Today the story is the same in every church where Christ's power is sought by Christ's people. As the church advances Christ's cause in the world, it does so successfully only under the guiding power of the Holy Spirit. His work will continue until the end of this age. *"Not by might nor by power, but by my Spirit,' says the LORD Almighty."*[4]

Does not your soul soar when you realize what an amazing movement God's Holy Spirit has invited you to join? Are you not delighted to know God has chosen you to be empowered with His Holy Spirit and to advance His work through you in this new day?

Our Strength: The Holy Spirit

An out-of-town couple leaving one of our Sunday morning worship services once said to me, "We come here every six weeks or so to worship because we feel the Holy Spirit's presence here."

To this we respond, "Praise God from whom all blessings flow!" The Holy Spirit is still very much involved in empowering Christ's life in us.

Christ's Spirit is present in every worship service for He said, *"Where two or three come together in my name, there am I with them."*[95] He heartens our singing: *"Sing and make music in your heart to the Lord."*[96]

The Holy Spirit empowers our preaching: *"Our gospel came to you not simply with words, but also with power, with the Holy Spirit and with deep conviction."*[97] He brings worship alive: *"For the letter kills, but the Spirit gives life."*[98] Worship without the Holy Spirit is dead. Worship in which the Holy Spirit is given freedom to do business for Christ is alive, vibrant, and life-transforming.

On Pentecost, a timid, frightened, confused group of direction-less disciples became dauntless, wise, strong leaders and preachers of Christ's cross, resurrection, and power for living. Wherever the Holy Spirit is at work He comforts the afflicted and afflicts the comfortable.

The Holy Spirit enables our profession of faith: *"No one can say, 'Jesus is Lord,' except by the Holy Spirit."*[99] He interprets our prayers. *"Because the Spirit intercedes for the saints in accordance with God's will."*[100]

The Holy Spirit empowers our work in Christ's name. *"It was he who gave some to be apostles, some to be prophets, some to be evangelists, and some to be pastors and teachers, to prepare God's people for works of service, so that the body of Christ may be built up."*[101]

The Holy Spirit is our teacher. He not only equips people to teach among us but He also gives life to their message. *"When he, the Spirit of truth, comes, he will guide you into all truth . . . He will bring glory to me by taking from what is mine and making it known to you."*[102]

The Power Who Points Us to Jesus

In all these areas of our life together in the church the Holy Spirit has one aim and only one. That aim is to point us to God's beloved Son with whom He is well pleased. The Spirit never draws attention to Himself but only to Jesus. In that alone will we find fulfillment in our relentless pursuit of excellence for Christ.

F. B. Meyer discovered that opening his entire life to the Holy Spirit enabled him to overcome a secret sin that had dogged his life for many years. After a long battle he prayed, "Lord, here are the keys to my life. Take them and unlock every door. Fill each room and make me willing to welcome You there." In response to that prayer God's Spirit moved in and through F. B. Meyer's life as never before. In the Spirit's power he was used in ways he had not previously dreamed. His ministry spread from London all across the world. Today, more than half a century after his death, he is still touching lives through the message of his forty books, tracts, and articles. His life is a splendid illustration of what God can do with all of us who open ourselves completely to Him. The same Holy Spirit will answer that prayer in each of us in ways that are good and exciting.

Does God's Holy Spirit have the keys to every room in your life? Someone asked Gipsy Smith how to start a revival in their church. "Go home," Gipsy Smith replied, "and lock yourself in your room. Kneel in the middle of the floor. Draw a chalk circle around yourself and ask God to start the revival inside that circle. When He does, the revival has started." Have you used any chalk recently?

As we dedicate ourselves to Christ and to working together, it will be our present and our future. Let every heart be open, and let us spend ourselves for Christ's kingdom in the power of the Holy Spirit. Working together in Him we can make a positive difference in this generation. Let revival come, O Holy Spirit, let it come quickly, and let it begin in me. In Jesus' name! Amen.

Themes to Think On - Things To Do

1. Who will you stand with, and who will stand with you as you accomplish your mission?

2. Make a list of important people who will play a vital role in fulfilling your mission. List what you expect of them and how you plan to support them. Now communicate this clearly to them.

GOOD ENOUGH ISN'T
GOOD ENOUGH!

Philippians 4:8
*"If anything is excellent or praiseworthy—
think about such things."*

〜〜〜〜

"It's close enough for government work," he said to his help-
er. That maybe true for the government, but this is no ordinary government housing. This is the house of the King of Kings.
I decided then and there this workman's handiwork deserved a
little closer inspection than I had perhaps planned to give it before. Sure enough, "close enough for government work" defined
a poor quality of workmanship on our church project from start
to finish. Corners were not square, gaps showed at door bottoms,
and windows were not sealed. For the man who did that work,
getting by was acceptable. He did not realize that good enough
simply is not good enough for God. What is more, he seemed not
to realize that his example would do nothing to inspire his young

assistant to try harder. Hence, the workman failed not only in achieving excellence, he failed also as a mentor. His unwillingness to reach for excellence may well produce inferior workmanship in generations still to come.

The Cult of Second Best

Good enough can be expensive in many ways. The loss of seven astronauts who perished aboard space shuttle Columbia when it disintegrated nearly forty miles above the Earth, stunned America and much of the rest of the world. It provided another of those moments that we will always remember where we were when we heard the news. It was an unspeakable tragedy. Tragically, the official investigation determined that it was a catastrophe that never should have happened. Investigators reported, among other things, that a culture of good enough had become the norm with NASA. Repeated take-off debris strikes on the orbiters became an accepted way of life along with such other decisions as cutting corners on maintenance under the assumption that the NASA shuttle fleet was nearing the end of its usefulness. These and other decisions to make do with less grew out of a get-by mentality. A culture of "good enough" to get by took over at NASA.[104] It was a horribly wrong and dreadfully expensive mentality for the families of the astronauts and for people around the world. A once proud organization, world renowned for putting a man on the moon, was brought to its knees. This is just one illustration of how "good enough" can never be an acceptable way of doing things.

This chapter calls us to recognize that good enough simply isn't good enough and this statement is never truer than when we are about God's business. *"Praise the LORD! Praise God in His sanctuary; Praise Him in His mighty expanse. Praise Him for His mighty deeds; Praise Him according to His excellent greatness."*[105] The message seems plain enough. If God has blessed us with excellence all throughout His creation, then surely we should use that as a model for our own praise.

Tragically, the same spirit of "good enough" which the construction worker tried to pass off that day prevails in the church. We have turned the church of the most high God into a cult where second best is acceptable. We celebrate mediocrity and wonder why many people consider us insignificant or why the church has lost its moral influence over society. "The society which scorns excellence in plumbing because plumbing is a humble activity and tolerates shoddiness in philosophy because it is an exalted activity will have neither good plumbing nor good philosophy. Neither its pipes nor its theories will hold water," declared John Gardner.[106] The fact remains that our society demands excellence in our appearance and our products—hence the billions of dollars that are invested annually into research and development by corporations of all sizes—yet in the church we often seem content to give second best.

EXCELLENCE!

"An excellent wife is the crown of her husband."[107] If this principle is true for the secular world, how much more so should Christ's bride—the church that bears His name—pursue excellence! Just what is excellence? And how can we cultivate a spirit of excellence in the church of Jesus Christ in the twenty-first century? In this chapter, I propose to look at excellence under three general

headings. First, a brief discussion of the meanings and uses of the words excellent and excellence in Scripture. Second, a word about how pastors might apply what the Bible says in their individual ministries. Third, how lay leaders might appropriate what Scripture says in their local church settings.

Excellence Defined

Both Old Testament Hebrew and New Testament Greek help us to discern what God has in mind when His word speaks about excellence or the quality of being excellent. The Hebrew, *gaon*, is chiefly related to the idea of swelling or growing greater. In a variety of forms, this word calls us to rise above the norm and is translated in a context that speaks of being above, of superabundance and surpassing elevation. One example is, *"To Him who rides upon the highest heavens, which are from ancient times; Behold, He speaks forth with His voice, a mighty voice. Ascribe strength to God; His majesty is over Israel; And His strength is in the skies."*[108] The idea is that God rises above the heavens, or literally "in heaven's heavens," that is, above all things. In the New Testament, the same idea is conveyed by the use of the Greek *perisseuo* and *huperecho*. In every instance, it speaks of going past the norm. Thus we can define excellence as going beyond the ordinary or as Booker T. Washington reportedly defined it for his students when he called them to excellence: "Excellence is to do a common thing in an uncommon way."[109] Our English words—*excel, excellent, excellence*—do not find their root in ancient Hebrew or Greek, but in the Latin word *excello*, meaning "to rise above, surpass."

One of Latin ancestry who understood the concept of *excello* was

Antonio Stradivari of Milan. For nearly four centuries, the Latinized version of his name, Stradivarius, has been synonymous with superior violins. Rare are those connoisseurs of fine musical instruments who do not agree that a Stradivarius is not the nearest thing to perfection that has ever been achieved in any musical instrument of any kind. And for good reason. Stradivari firmly resolved that no instrument of his would leave his shop until it was as near to perfection as human hands could make it. For him, being "good enough" was never good enough. Today, nearly four hundred years after he was born in Cremona, Milan, his instruments are the very definition of excellence; they are the standard by which other violins are measured. Once Stradivari is said to have observed, "God needs violins to send his music into the world and if any violins are defective then God's music will be spoiled." His philosophy of work was summed up in a simple phrase, "Other men will make other violins, but no man shall make a better one."[110] Antonio Stradivari knew the meaning of excellence—to do the ordinary in an extraordinary way, to rise above what others call acceptable.

Rising above the ordinary means rising before the ordinary and soaring above the ordinary morning at Paul Harvey's house in West Suburban River Forest near Chicago. The alarm clock rings at 3:30 a.m. and Paul Harvey's daily routine kicks in like clockwork: brush teeth, shower, shave, get dressed, eat oatmeal, get into car, and drive downtown. It all takes a well-organized forty-five minutes or so. Paul Harvey dresses formally to report for work—shirt, coat, and tie—not in the often slovenly manner common to many radio performers. "It is all about discipline," Harvey says. "I could go to work in my pajamas, but long ago I got some advice from the engineer for my friend Billy Graham's radio show. If you don't [use discipline] in every area, you'll lose your edge."[111] Paul Harvey sees himself as God's servant. He understands the idea of giving our best to the One who gave His Son for us. It is no wonder then that he chuckled as he delivered this:

The Butterball turkey company sets up a telephone hotline during the holidays to answer consumer questions about preparing turkeys. Once a woman called and asked about cooking a turkey that had been lying on her freezer bottom for twenty-three years! The Butterball representative told her the turkey would probably be safe to eat if the freezer had been kept below zero for the entire twenty-three years. But the Butterball representative admitted that even if the turkey were safe to eat, its flavor would likely have deteriorated so much that she would not recommend eating it. The caller replied, "That's what I thought. We'll give the turkey to our church!"

It was a case of giving something not good enough for her family to the family of God, a kind of modern Ananias and Sapphira story.[112]

"Whatever you do, work at it with all your heart, as working for the Lord, not for men, since you know that you will receive an inheritance from the Lord as a reward. It is the Lord Christ you are serving."[113] The recognition that all our work is an act of worship should inspire us to soar above drudgery and reach for our best in everything. This means striving tomorrow to be better than we were today and then striving the day after that to be better again. It calls for matching our performance with our potential. Excellence is never an accident. It only happens when we determine to make

it happen. People stumble into mediocrity but no one ever stumbles into excellence because excellence never happens by happenstance. The road to second best is easy to find. You can even find it without looking for a signpost and it is never far away. Excellence, on the other hand, is harder to achieve. We get there by the sweat of our brow over a long period of time. As Ted W. Engstrom says in his fine book, *The Pursuit of Excellence*, "All excellence involves discipline and tenacity of purpose."[114] Paul Harvey knows this. That's why—even in his eighties—he still sets that alarm clock for 3:30 every morning.

A word of caution is in order here. Excellence and perfection are not synonyms. To pursue perfection is different from pursuing excellence. Chasing after perfection can, and often does, result in neurosis and frustration. Going after excellence, on the other hand, is a healthy thing, a good exercise for mind and body. When perfection is achieved, the result will sometimes be a sense of despair because there are no more mountains to climb. Alexander the Great, for example, supposedly wept when he realized there were no more worlds to conquer. On the other hand, when excellence is achieved there is a sense of accomplishment and gratification.

Nor is excellence about being the best. It is about giving your best. If it were about being the best, then there would be only one excellent person in every profession, one excellent church in God's kingdom, one excellent preacher in all the world. When you are the best at something, the reality is that there is only one way to go and it's down. When it is excellence you are after, the only way is up.

EXCELLENCE IN MINISTRY

"Praise the LORD in song, for He has done excellent things; Let this be known throughout the earth."[115] There is finally only one way for the church to tell the news of God's excellence throughout the earth and that is for us to resolve to give Him nothing short of our best (as opposed to "the" best). We must come to realize that mediocrity has never yet inspired anyone to do anything worthwhile. The good news is that we can choose whether we will settle for half-hearted mediocrity or strive for excellence. Like that workman at the church, we can determine whether we become mediocre handymen or enthusiastic craftsmen in the pursuit of excellence. Excellence is far more about habit than results. It is a day-by-day determination to rise above what you were before and to become what you can be. That calls for perseverance and commitment. People who are dedicated to the pursuit of excellence have in common the commitment to constant change and constant improvement. The whole quality of our lives will be directly in proportion to our commitment to excellence, regardless of our field of endeavor. People who produce good results always feel good about themselves and they constantly amaze themselves by what they do. It all begins at the point of choosing and our choice will bear witness to our attitude. Someone has said that no one ever died from overwork but many have died from under-motivation. Surely the saddest people of all at the end of life are those who step out into eternity knowing they have offered up something less than their best and now it is too late to make amends.

DROP OUT VERSUS COP OUT

"'May the LORD, the God of the spirits of all mankind, appoint a man over this community to go out and come in before them, one who will lead

them out and bring them in, so the LORD's people will not be like sheep without a shepherd.' So the LORD said to Moses, 'Take Joshua son of Nun, a man in whom is the spirit, and lay your hand on him.'"[116] These words come at one of the most important moments in Israel's history. A new day is dawning. Moses, knowing that his time is short, does not want to leave his sheep without a shepherd. He asks God to appoint a leader to lead both the internal and external affairs of the children of Israel. God's response to Moses' prayer is Joshua, *"a man in whom is the spirit."* I believe a fair paraphrase could say, "a man in whom is the desire to lead the people to a new level." In short, Joshua would not be satisfied with status quo.

Excellence begins with a willing heart. The first call for a leader who would be excellent is to have this spirit of giving the best he or she is capable of giving. The spirit of excellence never enters any organization until it first possesses the leader. Down through the ages, this has been the case among those God has used to maximize their impact on His work and influence the future direction of His people. And it never has been more vital than in these first days of the third millennium. This is what the Twenty-first Century demands of its pastors and preachers. That is, a desire for excellence—excellence in faith and commitment. Not excuse! Not complaint! Not compromise! Not a willingness to get by with second best!

The New York Times reports that faith is fading fast among European Roman Catholics.[117] A primary reason cited is the failure of the Catholic Church in Europe to attract new priests. The shortage has reached crisis levels. In fact, it is not European Catholics alone who struggle with this shortage. Every mainline denomination in

America suffers from the same dilemma. Denominations wrestle with the so-called "problem of the empty pulpits" and there seems to be no relief in sight. The implication is that we have a numbers problem. That is, if we had sufficient numbers of pastors for those "empty pulpits" this dilemma would disappear.

I am convinced that a greater problem is the pulpits that appear to be filled but are, in fact, vacant because they lack not a warm body but the very same spirit that was in Joshua. We do not need more pastors. We need better pastors filled with Joshua's spirit. To much is made of clergy burnout. It is a serious problem and will likely become increasingly so as the ratio of pastors to congregations continues to decline. I know about it firsthand. I also see it among some friends. However, I see more of what I call "Lazy Pastor Syndrome." There are too many pastors who will rust out long before they burn out simply because they lack the commitment to put in the hours and pour out the energy necessary to advance the kingdom where they serve. No longer soaring eagles, they have become lifeless turkeys wandering aimlessly from day to day in a land of promise.

I once heard the late Bill Bright, founder of Campus Crusade for Christ, tell a story about an eagle that thought it was a barnyard chicken. Hence it spent its life walking around a barnyard, eating the grit and gravel below it. One day a beautiful eagle flew above it, soaring on wings directed by the wind. The bird looked up for a moment and said, "I wish I could soar like that, but I can't for I'm just a barnyard chicken." But, he wasn't! He was an eagle and he needed only to look again at who he was created to be and try his wings. That eagle reminds me of many pastors I meet.

Theirs is not a problem of overwork but of low expectation. They do not expect much, nor do they have a burning desire for their churches to rise to new heights of greatness. As a result, not much happens there that is exciting. It is a problem that begins with attitude. Too many pastors I know are retreating behind ecclesiastical committees, biding their time until retirement or some "better opportunity" comes their way. Theirs is no longer a call from God. It is a job and a chore. They fail to realize that the best opportunity we have—indeed, the only opportunity we have—is the one we have where we are today.

These *"watchmen of uncertain trumpets"*[118] settle for preaching that is dull, dreary, lifeless, and unexciting. It neither seeks nor builds a spirit of enthusiasm (the word means "in-God-ism") among the people to whom it is addressed. Hence it is no wonder that the number of people who experience a personal sense of call under their ministries is virtually non-existent. Others seem to be more interested in building careers than building the congregations where they are right now. The call of the hour is for a new sense of call; for pastors who will view pastoral ministry not as a job but as an urgent response to God's summons; pastors full of Joshua's spirit, who are willing to stop counting hours and seeking glory for themselves and give ministry their best efforts. Our challenge is not clergy drop out but clergy cop out! My prayer as I write these words is that they will ignite a new desire for excellence in pulpits and among pastors wherever they are read. When that happens, however it happens, pastoral ministry will be revived again and the ranks of the pastors will grow. It will only happen when we as pastors recommit ourselves to reach higher than we are or have been; that is, reach up for excellence. I find in my own ministry that it begins each Sunday evening. That is when I begin to zero in on my message for the coming week. Having done most of my advance planning and research over the preceding months, now the challenge is to make sure that the message I deliver to God's people next Sunday morning will be better than the one I delivered that morning, better than any I have brought them before.

As Tom Peters and Nancy Austin remind us in *A Passion for Excellence: The Leadership Difference,* excellence begins with thinking big. It grows out of a burning desire to do our best. It also demands a price and is not for the faint of heart. To settle for less than giving our best should really "bother us."[119]

How will that happen in your life and ministry? It will not happen without prayer and it will not occur without taking God's Word seriously. It calls for determination to rise above the ordinary, to keep going after others quit. Neither will it happen in the hearts of the people God entrusts to my pastoral care until it happens in my heart. It can begin today as we resolve to rise above what we have been and become more like the pastors God made us to be. We must each personalize the psalmist's prayer, *"Will you not revive us again, that your people may rejoice in you?"*[120] If we will inspire the church to excellence, we pastors must first reach for excellence in our own lives. Let us settle for nothing less.

WHEN GOOD ENOUGH SIMPLY ISN'T GOOD ENOUGH IN THE PEWS

Not long ago I asked a group of church leaders how many of them would allow threadbare, frazzled-edge carpet—like the

one that for years covered the floor of their otherwise spectac-
ular sanctuary—lie in their own homes. "How many of you," I
quizzed them, "have carpet in this condition on the floors of your
home?" No one answered. Next I asked, "How many of you have
thrown away better carpet than this from your own homes?" Several raised their hands. Of the twenty or so people who heard my
question, not one said such carpet would be acceptable in their
homes. One elder, perhaps suspecting where my questions were
leading them, protested my approach. "What would your wife
say," I asked him, "If you were to bring this carpet home today
and tell her that you planned to install it in the living room?"

"She wouldn't let either it or me in the door," he admitted.

"Yet," I responded, "you and your fellow elders have apparently
decided that carpet like this is good enough for God's house!"

He may not have liked my comeback but I think he began to get
the point. All too often as I visit around churches, unchallenged
church members and leaders treat God's house as a hand-me-down
center for furniture, office equipment, and other items that they
have decided are no longer good enough for their business offices or
homes. Items that are no longer in good working order or that have
been replaced by much improved new models in our business offices
are often given to the church of Jesus Christ. Worse still, they are
accepted with at least feigned gratitude by mealy-mouthed pastors
and church leaders. The spirit of Ananias and Sapphira is still alive
in many places in the church of the new millennium! Something
is seriously wrong when we try to palm off anything less than our
absolute best to the One who gave His best for us on Calvary and

"called us by His own glory and excellence."[121] Whatever happened to "Give of your best to the Master"? The issue is excellence. Anything short of excellence is mediocrity or worse.

It is not the pastors alone who must work to bring about a renewed spirit of excellence in the church. The laity, too, must rise to newness of spirit if we are to know revival. In fact, without a determination to reach for excellence from the pews, any attempt to do so from the pulpits will likely be short-lived. The laity must come to see and acknowledge that the church is simply losing its impact in the world.

"Moses' hands were heavy. Then they took a stone and put it under him, and he sat on it; and Aaron and Hur supported his hands, one on one side and one on the other. Thus his hands were steady until the sun set."[122] God used Dale Bogard to save my ministry, perhaps even to save my life. At a critical point, when it looked as though the enemies of renewal at the church I was serving might succeed in ending my ministry, Dale came to my office unannounced one evening when I was especially low. He said, "I'm here for one reason and it's to hold up your arms." He remembered how Aaron and Hur stood by Moses' side and held up his arms to bring about the victory against Amalek. Dale decided God was calling him to do the same thing for his pastor. Not long ago, Dale was called home to heaven, but I could never have repaid him for the inspiration his presence and words brought me at a time of spiritual lowness that bordered on defeat. It was a critical moment, but God, through Dale, let me know that I was not alone in the battle and that I was loved. When love comes into the picture, especially in times of discouragement, it presents to the world an indisputable

mark of a true follower of Jesus Christ and a force that will never be overcome. As a result, a special bond developed between us. There was nothing I would not do for him and there was nothing he could say that would offend me. In the months and years that followed, Dale came to me with suggestions and corrections many times. Because of him, I am a better pastor and a better man. He helped me in the pursuit of excellence.

I am convinced that every pastor needs a Dale Bogard in his or her life—to bring a word of encouragement or inspiration, offer support in prayer, or walk beside the pastor in troubled times. I am convinced that had Dale not come that evening and offered to hold up my arms, I would have become totally discouraged and lost the battle. Furthermore, I am convinced that every pastor will benefit from the support and loving direction of the laity. You do understand, don't you, that God has given the church and its pastors an overwhelming assignment for this new millennium? We are called to take the redemptive word of Christ's cross to a new generation. It is a generation that does not always welcome God's Word, one that sees a lot of reasons to have little or nothing to do with the church as it knows it.

No pastor can accomplish this task alone. Pastors need the Holy Spirit to inspire, lead, and empower them. That will happen often through lay people who are ready to stand with their pastors in this battle for the hearts and souls of people both inside and outside the church. What the church needs now are not more and more people but better and better people. Jesus Christ called out twelve to walk especially close to Him. One of those was a dud but through the other eleven and their spiritual offspring, God started a fire in Jerusalem that has never gone out and never will. Our call as pastors and laity alike is to burn the flame ever brighter by committing ourselves to better serving Him in His church every single day for the rest of our lives. What the church needs is a determined pursuit of excellence and it will come nearer to finding it when you resolve that you will reach higher to do your best.

What can you, as a layperson do to inspire excellence in your church and in your pastor? Following are some suggestions:

You can come to see unity as a special gift from God.

Recognize the call of your pastor as sacred—a treasure to be valued—and challenge your pastor to lead you to new heights with Christ.

Ask yourself what obstacles to excellence exist in your church and work with all your heart to help your pastor to overcome them.

Commit yourself to affirming your pastor when he or she does something worthy of praise and gently correct him or her when you feel he or she is not delivering his or her best for Christ.

Make sure that ample provision of time and financial support is made for your pastor to have an opportunity for rest and spiritual refreshment and make sure that the pastor takes full advantage of such opportunities.

Determine that you will speak only well of the pastor and that, where necessary, you will do all in your power to quench detractors, gossips, and unfair critics.

Resolve with God's help that you will personally reach for new levels of excellence in your own spiritual life.

Steward your life in such a way as to allow time each day to pray for a renewed spirit of excellence to enter your church and resolve with God's help to do everything in your power to make it come to pass.

"Just as you excel in everything—in faith, in speech, in knowledge, in complete earnestness and in your love for us—see that you also excel in this grace of giving."[123] Let us be careful not to quickly jump only to the financial aspects of these words. To be sure, they speak to Christian stewardship but they are far more than that alone. The Corinthian Christians excelled in all things, whether faith, speech (preaching), learning, sincerity, or love. Theirs was a case of excellence in all things. Whether clergy or lay leader, the reality is that there are no good alternatives to excellence. Either a thing is excellent or it is mediocre, second best, sub-standard, or good enough. But good enough is not good enough for the One who gave His all for us that we might live life in abundance. Whether clergy or laity, we are challenged throughout Scripture to go above and beyond and do our utmost for God's kingdom. There is no higher calling than the relentless pursuit of excellence for Christ. Anything less just is not good enough.

ENDNOTES

1. Mark 12:30
2. Philippians 2:6-9
3. John 21:16-18
4. Revelation 3:20
5. John 17:17
6. see Isaiah 40:3 & Isaiah 7:14
7. see Micah 5:2
8. Nahum 1:14
9. Isaiah 13:19
10. Daniel 4:37
11. see Isaiah 33:20
12. see Jeremiah 39:8
13. Daniel 9:25
14. Micah 7:11
15. Matthew 4:4,6,10
16. John 5:39,40
17. John 8:58
18. Matthew 28:18
19. Mark 13:31
20. Matthew 28:20
21. John 8:46
22. John 5:22
23. Luke 5:20
24. John 10:30

25. John 14:6

26. Isaiah 7:14

27. see Matthew 1:18-25

28. Psalm 16:8-10

29. see Luke 24:5-7

30. Psalm 68:18

31. see Ephesians 4:8-10

32. John Stuart Mill, *Fidelis* (volume 3, chapter 26)

33. Stephen Vincent Benet poem, *Young Adventure*

34. I John 2:1,2

35. Isaiah 53:4,5

36. see Galatians 2:20

37. Matthew 16:18

38. Exodus 20:4

39. Galatians 6:14

40. I Corinthians 1:21

41. Acts 2:24

42. Psalm 16:9

43. Philippians 3:10

44. John 11:25

45. John 14:19

46. Romans 1:4

47. Revelation 1:18

48. Joel 2:25

49. II Corinthians 12:9

50. John 14:19

51. John 13:23

52. I Corinthians 13:12

53. Genesis 6:16

54. John 3:16

55. I Corinthians 13:1

56. Ephesians 1:4

57. Romans 5:11

58. Ephesians 2:8-10

59. I Corinthians 1:18

60. Romans 6:14

61. Romans 7:19

62. Romans 5:9

63. Romans 8:30

64. Acts 4:12

65. I Peter 4:10,11

66. Hebrews 4:15

67. John 15:4

68. II Thessalonians 1:11

69. II Thessalonians 1:3

70. II Thessalonians 1:3

71. John 13:35

72. II Thessalonians 1:4

73. Philippians 1:29

74. II Thessalonians 1:5

75. II Thessalonians 1:6

76. II Corinthians 5:9

77. Galatians 2:20

78. I John 4:19

79. John 3:16

80. Acts 1:8

81. Deuteronomy 6:4

82. Deuteronomy 6:4

83. Psalm 139:7-12

84. John 14:16, 17

85. Acts 13:2,3

86. Genesis 1:1,2

87. Genesis 1:9

88. Luke 1:35

89. Luke 4:18,19

90. Hebrews 9:14

91. Acts 1:8

92. Matthew 16:18

93. Acts 1:8

94. Zechariah 4:6

95. Matthew 18:20

96. Ephesians 5:19

97. I Thessalonians 1:5

98. II Corinthians 3:6

99. I Corinthians 12:13

100. Romans 8:27

101. Ephesians 4:11-12

102. John 16:13-15

103. Philippians 4:8

104. Orlando Sentinel online edition, June 6, 2003,
     Report on Shuttle Accident to Slam NASA Decisions, Culture

105. Psalm 150:1,2

106. *Leadership Journal*, volume 4, no.3

107. Proverbs 12:4

108. Psalm 68:33,34

109. *Holy Sweat*, Tim Hansel (Word, 1987), p. 111

110. *Our Daily Bread*, published by RBC Ministries, Grand Rapids, MI 49555, January 25,1993

111. Kogan, Rick, *Good Days for Paul Harvey*, Chicago Tribune Magazine, August 4, 2002, p. 10

112. Adapted from Paul Harvey News broadcast, November 22, 1995

113. Colossians 3:23,24

114. Engstrom, Ted W., *The Pursuit of Excellence*, Grand Rapids, MI, Zondervan, 1982, p.24

115. Isaiah 12:5

116. Numbers 27:16-18

117. New York Times online edition, October 13, 2003

118. see Ezekial 33:6,7

119. Peters, Tom and Nancy Austin, *A Passion for Excellence: The Leadership Difference*, New York: Random House (1985), pp. 414-415

120. Psalm 85:6

121. II Peter 1:3

122. Exodus 17:12

123. II Corinthians 8:7

Index